A PLACE IN
THE ROCKS

Published by the Historic Houses Trust of New South Wales
The Mint, 10 Macquarie Street, Sydney NSW 2000, Australia
www.hht.net.au

© 2008 Historic Houses Trust of New South Wales

The Historic Houses Trust is a statutory authority of, and principally funded by, the NSW State Government. The Trust conserves, manages and interprets important properties and house museums in New South Wales for the education and enjoyment of the public. Properties of the Trust include: Elizabeth Bay House, Elizabeth Farm, Government House, Hyde Park Barracks Museum, Justice & Police Museum, Meroogal, Museum of Sydney on the site of first Government House, Rose Seidler House, Rouse Hill House & Farm, Susannah Place Museum, The Mint and Caroline Simpson Library & Research Collection, and Vaucluse House.

This book is copyright. Apart from any fair dealing for the purpose of private study, research, criticism or review, as permitted under the Copyright Act, no part of this publication may be reproduced for any purpose without written permission.

Design: Anne-Louise Falson
Editorial: Vani Sripathy and Rhiain Hull
Picture rights and permissions: Alice Livingstone
Pre-press by Spitting Image, Sydney
Printed by Imago Productions, Singapore

National Library of Australia Cataloguing-in-Publication data:
Cossu, Anna.
A place in The Rocks.
ISBN 978 1 876991 28 9 (pbk.).

1. Historic sites – New South Wales – Rocks, The. 2. Susannah Place (Sydney, N.S.W.) – History. 3. Rocks, The (Sydney, N.S.W.) – Buildings, structures, etc. 4. Rocks, The (Sydney, N.S.W.) – History. I. Historic Houses Trust of New South Wales. II. Title.
994.41

Transcripts for all oral histories referred to in this book are held at Susannah Place Museum. Original recordings of the oral histories are held by Caroline Simpson Library & Research Collection, Historic Houses Trust.

Front cover flap quote from Cedric Flower & John Carnemolla, The Rocks, Horwitz, Sydney, 1969, Introduction.

Picture credits front cover The Rocks and Harbour Bridge, Sali Herman, 1970, oil on canvas. Private collection, South Australia. © Estate of the artist. Photograph courtesy Deutscher-Menzies **back cover** Rear, No 64 Gloucester Street, photograph © Christopher Shain, 1995 **back cover flap** © Stephen Baccon/Fairfaxphotos **p4** (from left) Kristine and Jeffrey Smith with their mother, Beryl. Jenni Whitford (girl in centre looking down) and Maria Murdoch (seated) in the back lane (Cambridge Street). c1960s. Courtesy Jenni Whitford; Front door, No 58 Gloucester Street, photograph © Ross Heathcote, 2004; Jenni Whitford (right) hosting a tea party for friend Maria Murdoch in back lane, c1960s. Courtesy Jenni Whitford; Front door, No 60 Gloucester Street, photograph © Ross Heathcote, 2007; Simon Ford outside No 64 Gloucester St, c1980s. Courtesy Jenni Whitford **p5** (from left) Front door, No 62 Gloucester Street, photograph © Ross Heathcote, 2004; Luke and Louella Ford (grandchildren of Ellen Marshall) outside No 62 Gloucester Street, c1980s. Courtesy Ellen Marshall; Front door, No 64 Gloucester Street, photograph © Ross Heathcote, 2007; Jack Andersen with his grandfather, John Gallagher, c1940s. Courtesy Terri Williams **p6** Back gate, No 64 Gloucester Street, photograph © Ross Heathcote, 2007.

All Ross Heathcote and Christopher Shain photographs of Susannah Place owned by Susannah Place Museum Collection, Historic Houses Trust.

A PLACE IN THE ROCKS

Anna Cossu

Generously supported by the Governors Program
FOUNDATION FOR THE HISTORIC HOUSES TRUST

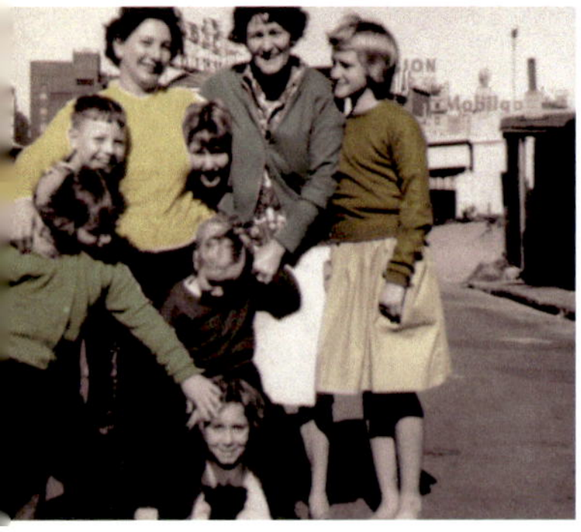

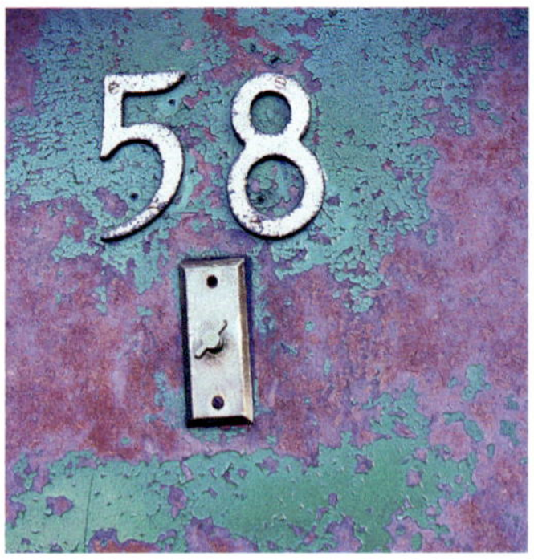
58

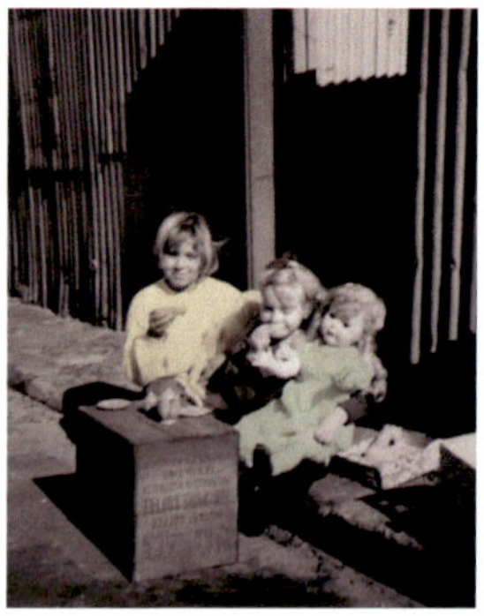

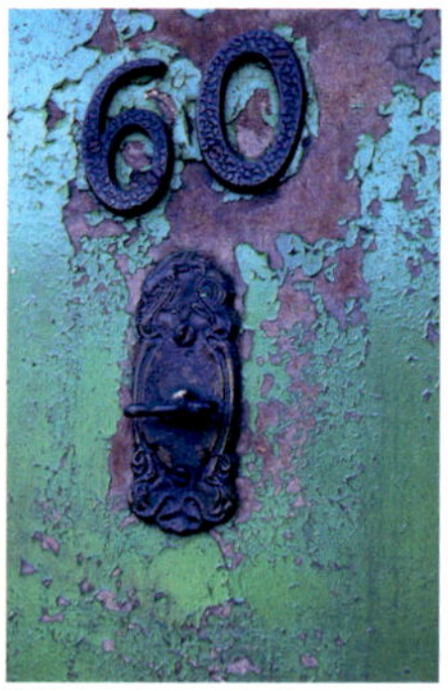
60

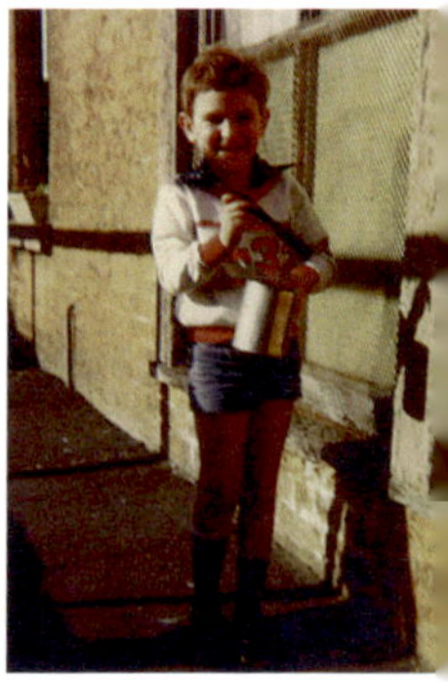

CONTENTS

	Foreword	7
1	Words on The Rocks	8
2	From the ground up	34
3	Around the block	60
4	Making a mark	86
5	Shared history, separate lives	112
	Tenants list	142
	Further reading	144
	Acknowledgments	144

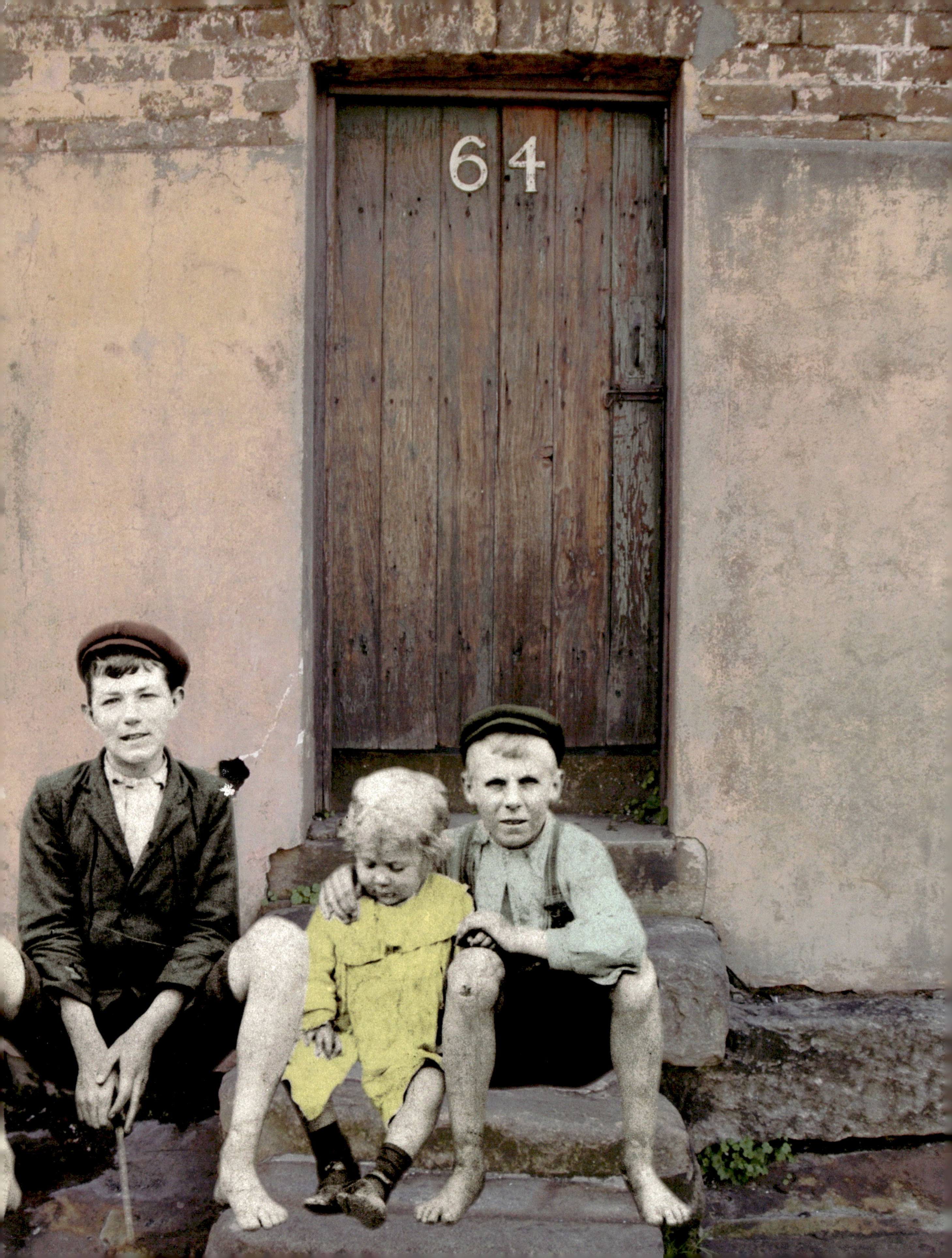
64

FOREWORD

Susannah Place breaks the mould of most house museums, for it tells the stories, not of the wealthy and prominent, but of the often overlooked and everyday lives of ordinary people. When I first visited Susannah Place in the early 1980s its modest exterior and battered and layered interiors hinted at the richness of its hidden stories. Built in 1844 by Irish immigrants and continuously occupied until 1990, this typically English terrace has now had those stories gently coaxed from its past.

The Historic Houses Trust's involvement with Susannah Place began in the mid 1980s when the then Chairman of the Trust, Jack Ferguson, a former Deputy Premier of New South Wales and long time Minister for Public Works became concerned that the 'real' character of The Rocks was fast disappearing in the rush to redevelop and restore. He searched for a project that would continue to tell the real story of The Rocks and its people. At that time three of the four houses that form Susannah Place had been vacant since the early 1970s and required urgent conservation work. With Jack Ferguson's encouragement a joint project was formed between the owners, the Sydney Cove Authority (now the Sydney Harbour Foreshore Authority), and the Historic Houses Trust to conserve as much as possible of the original building and the changes made by successive tenants and their landlords, and to allow it to tell its own stories.

In 1993 the terrace was opened to the public as a 'museum in the making', allowing visitors the opportunity to see and respond to the incremental process of creating a museum in these modest dwellings. Since the opening of Susannah Place, many curators – Peter Emmett, Ann Toy, Robert Griffin, Sally Webster, Gary Crockett and, since 2004, Anna Cossu – have contributed to the ongoing development of the museum. Initial research established the names and occupations of the tenants. Ongoing research has allowed us to gradually re-create the lives of individual families who called Susannah Place home. Almost 15 years later new stories are still emerging and we are indebted to the former tenants, their families and descendants for sharing them with us.

Utilising an array of photographs, both public and private, this book takes us on a journey through The Rocks, along its streets and into the lives of those who lived in Nos 58, 60, 62 and 64 Gloucester Street. Anna Cossu has been the conduit through which the stories of Susannah Place have been learned and retold. She has played a major part in the life of the terrace, quietly absorbing its spirit, listening as its walls whispered their secrets, and gently coaxing out its ghosts. This is her story of the place that she continues to care for with such tenderness and integrity. It is beautifully told and we are indebted to Anna for her skill and her sensitivity.

Peter Watts AM
Director,
Historic Houses Trust

Known by the name of 'the rocks'; and which, from the ruggedness of its surface, the difficulty of access to it, and the total absence of order in its houses, was for many years more like the abode of a horde of savages than the residence of a civilised community.[1]

William C Wentworth, 1819

WORDS

1

ON THE ROCKS

Within days of the First Fleet's arrival at Sydney Cove in January 1788, the convicts and their guards and, later, the colony's first hospital and prison, occupied the rocky sandstone hills on the western side of the cove that became known as The Rocks. The landscape there was marked by a series of sandstone ridges that rose 'like steps of stairs' from the harbour to the top of the ridge to what is now Observatory Hill:

> *The portion of the town to the right is best known by the name of The Rocks, from the ridge whereon it is built being nothing more than a bare mass of white sandstone, often rising in successive layers (like steps of stairs) from the bottom to the top of the ridge.*[2]

The Rocks did not develop in an orderly fashion and much has been written about the unruly nature of its houses and people. Not everyone was enamoured with the new settlement. Reverend Johnson wrote in a letter home:

> *[I] give you it as my humble opinion Government would act very wisely to send out another fleet to take us all back to England, or to some other place more likely to answer than this poor wretched Country, where scarcely anything is to be seen but Rocks, or eaten but Rats.*[3]

Commissioner Bigge, sent out from England in 1819 to inquire into the colony's social and economic conditions, was equally scathing. He reported that the improvement found in Sydney architecture was marred by 'the irregular accumulation of houses that has gradually been formed in that part of it that is called the Rocks'.[4] Bigge found The Rocks to be a black spot on the otherwise well-behaved town of Sydney: 'with the exception of that part of town called the Rocks, the tranquillity of the streets was well maintained, and instances of open or public outrage were not frequent'.[5]

The first houses in The Rocks were indeed crudely built, stairs were carved straight out of the rocks, and rudimentary streets were linked with roughly established tracks. Convicts and their first generation of Australian-born children occupied the houses and within a few short years sailors and whalers from around the world took lodgings in the boarding houses and pubs that mushroomed in the area. Close to the water, merchants like Robert Campbell set up warehouses and stores to house the ever-increasing volume of goods coming into the colony. The Rocks area was built and rebuilt throughout the 19th century, as the early timber houses made way for more solid brick and sandstone buildings.

View of Sydney from east side of the cove (detail), John Eyre, 1810, hand-coloured aquatint, Mitchell Library, State Library of New South Wales **previous page** *Sydney from Pinchgut Island* (detail), Augustus Earle, 1826, hand coloured lithograph, Mitchell Library, State Library of New South Wales

The shore on each side is bounded by rocks ... The marines and convicts are to be encamped on the west side, and the Governor and staff, with his guard ... on the east side ...[6]

Lieutenant Philip Gidley King, 1788

Governor Macquarie renamed all the streets of Sydney in 1810, to bring a degree of 'ornament and regularity' to the town.[7] It seems strange in a country that abounds with borrowed names from Britain that the area considered to be the birthplace of white Australia escaped the governor's decree and retained a name as ordinary as 'The Rocks'. The reason may be traced to the very early days of the colony, before the formation and official naming of streets, when directions were given with reference to a local landmark, feature of the landscape or person who lived nearby. Early paintings show houses perched on the rocks with narrow tracks linking them to the main thoroughfare of High Street (now George Street).

Thus, a business or house located on the western side of the cove was described as being 'on the Rocks'. William Bowen's lost dog notice requested the finder return 'Tinker' to his 'residence on the Rocks'.[8] Rosetta Stabler's advertisement relied on the community's knowledge of the former occupant of her premises:

NEW EATING-HOUSE – VICTUALS DRESSED IN THE ENGLISH WAY.
At the House formerly occupied by Michael Knowland, near New Windmill, on the Rocks. ROSETTA STABLER respectfully acquaints the Public that she prepares Boiled Mutton and Broths every day at 12 o'clock, and a Joint of Meat Roasted always ready at One, which, from its quality and mode of serving, she flatters herself will attract the Notice of the Public.[9]

'The Rocks' first appeared in print in the *Sydney Gazette* on 5 March 1803. For it to have been published suggests the name had passed into common usage with the general population of the town. Yet for Aboriginal people the area already had a name. The Cadigal people called Sydney Cove *Warrane* and The Rocks, specifically the flat area by the water where the hospital was situated, was named *Tallawoladah*. For thousands of years the area provided the Cadigal with an abundance of food and a supply of fresh water.[10] A 1989 excavation at Cumberland Street uncovered a 500-year-old campfire with the remains of a meal of snapper, bream and rock oysters.

Governor Phillip's choice of Sydney Cove for his settlement was based on his belief that the harbour had 'the best spring of water' and that ships could 'anchor so close to the shore that at a very small expence [sic] quays may be made at which the largest ships may unload'.[11]

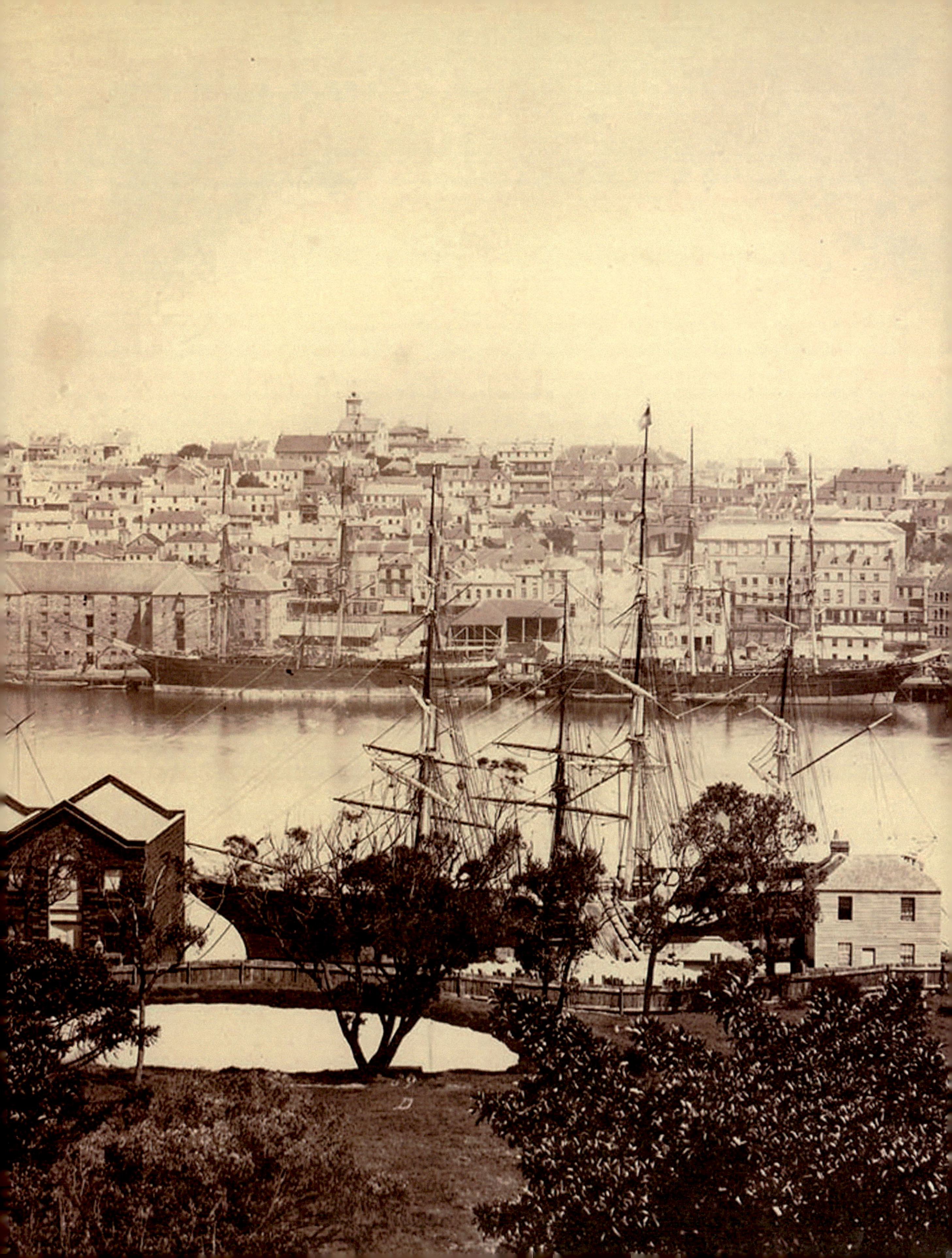

14

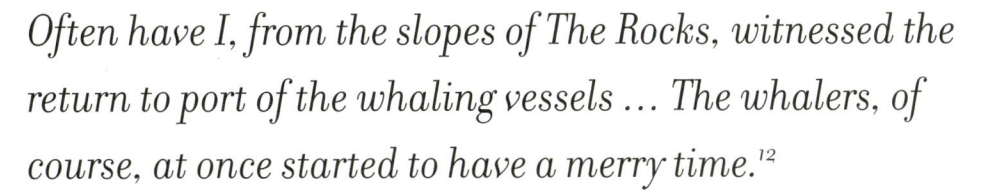

Often have I, from the slopes of The Rocks, witnessed the return to port of the whaling vessels ... The whalers, of course, at once started to have a merry time.[12]

Eliza Walker, 1901, resident of The Rocks in the 1840s

Surgeon White described the harbour as 'without exception, the finest and most extensive harbour in the universe and at the same time the most secure, being safe from all the winds that blow'.[13]

The harbour has remained a constant in the often turbulent history of The Rocks. It has 'influenced both the physical appearance of the area and the social and economic characteristics of its residents'.[14] Its deep anchorages have provided an ideal port for ships from around the world to unload their cargo, and by the 1820s goods such as whale oil, sealskins and wool were being exported from Sydney. The busy waterfront required a readily available workforce to service the ships, and with few transport options available, The Rocks soon became densely populated with maritime workers and their families. As one resident reminisced, 'If you didn't work at the waterfront you didn't work anywhere ... everyone worked at the waterfront'.[15]

Taking advantage of the thousands of sailors who landed in the area after their long months at sea were the area's numerous public houses. While Eliza Walker, who spent her childhood in The Rocks in the 1840s, paints a picture of merriment, Alexander Harris's description of the scenes he found at The Sheer Hulk and The Black Dog are of a different character entirely: 'We found it ... full of the lowest women, sailors and ruffians, who supported themselves by waylaying and robbing ... any intoxicated sea officer, newly-arrived emigrant, or up-country settler'.[16] These wild scenes were obviously not too off-putting as Harris returned to The Sheer Hulk on a number of occasions.

Wealthy colonists had established grand houses in The Rocks along Cumberland and Princes streets and in the area known as Bunker's Hill. By the 1850s, coinciding with the end of transportation to New South Wales, social conditions were beginning to change and The Rocks,

The Whalers Arms, Gloucester Street, The Rocks, 1901, Government Printing Office, albumen photoprint, Small Picture File collection, Mitchell Library, State Library of New South Wales

RLAND & GLOUCESTER STS

with its convict connections, rowdy pubs, overcrowded houses and working-class populace, was looked upon with disdain. Social scientist William Stanley Jevons made many observations of the area as he wandered the streets of Sydney in 1858, peering into windows, walking the streets and laneways, taking notes and pronouncing judgments:

> *I am acquainted with some of the worst parts of London ... and with the most unhealthy parts of Liverpool, Paris and other towns but nowhere have I seen such a retreat for filth & vice as 'the Rocks' of Sydney.*[17]

Although many observers' accounts have portrayed the housing in The Rocks as slums, the artefacts left behind by tenants often reveal a more complex story. Observing an ambiguity between the condition of houses and the archaeological material uncovered, archaeologist Wendy Thorp believed that the people lived within two environments: the 'environment of circumstance' that was beyond their control and the 'environment of choice'.[18]

Since very few working-class people owned the houses they lived in, they depended on their absentee landlords for the upkeep of the properties. Thorp concluded that 'the most practical response' to the uncontrollable external environment was to focus on the internal, creating a 'comfortable and interesting' space within and separate from the walls that surrounded them.[19]

Between 1851 and 1881 the population of The Rocks had almost doubled,[20] and the overcrowded living conditions were exacerbated by inadequate water and sewerage facilities. In 1851 a series of newspaper articles strongly condemned the sanitary conditions of Sydney,[21] a view propounded by the 1859 Select Committee on the Condition of the Working Classes, which described the overcrowding in the area:

> *I have never seen such a miserable class of houses as that on The Rocks. I know two or three houses which are not larger than this room, two or three families living in one house, perhaps partitioned off by boards; and for each of these partitions six shillings or eight shillings a week is charged.*[22]

Yet an alternative impression of dignity and a strong sense of neighbourhood and community also emerge from the area's residents. Eliza Walker had a high regard for its people and businesses: 'The Rocks could boast of being the abiding place of very many highly respectable families' and was home to 'the houses of many respectable working people'.[23]

The outbreak of bubonic plague in 1900 once again focused attention on the living conditions of the working class and became the catalyst for the government's resumption of the area. At a cost of £1,500,000 and as part of a massive slum clearance program,[24] hundreds of houses were demolished, tonnes of rubbish burnt or taken away, and new workers housing built in The Rocks and in neighbouring Millers Point. Yet, ten years on an article titled 'The tragedy of "the Rocks": a peep into Sydney's slum area' declared that The Rocks had reverted back to its 'old state of dirt-horror!' Promoting the Town Planning Association's agenda of urban renewal, the article was scathing about the buildings and people and set out to show 'how criminals are being bred out of the congestion and the darkness':

> What a hollow gibbering mockery of our vaunted Christianity; what a contradiction of our democracy; what an outrage on our twentieth century civilisation is the Sydney 'Rocks' area! … If you have a stout heart go and see for yourself — not the chaotic buildings, and the higgledy-piggledy streets so much, as the appearance of the dwellers in the darkness! … Man is the product of his environment: and like begets like — or worse.[25]

Much of what has been written about The Rocks comes from outsiders looking in. Historian Alan Mayne points out that these descriptions by middle-class observers and 'dabblers in social reform' were 'coloured by the lack of similarity between their own way of life' and the living conditions found in the working-class areas of the city.[26] Rocks people themselves, according to historian Peter Emmett, 'were suspicious of black-suited visitors: health inspectors, debt collectors, and urban missionaries saving souls'.[27]

Long-time Rocks residents like Fred Hughes were aware that while they 'weren't rich, just average', they were 'never crook on living there at all'.[28] For his sister Bertha, who also grew up in the area, the neighbourhood was familiar and safe; she knew the residents and they knew her: 'If I was coming home from a dance and walking through the Cut, late at night, as long as I saw one of the boys from the Point, I was safe'.[29] However it was a different story for outsiders.

Ellen Brennan (nee Cunninghame), c1900. Tenant No 60 Gloucester Street, 1845–46. Courtesy Tony Gye

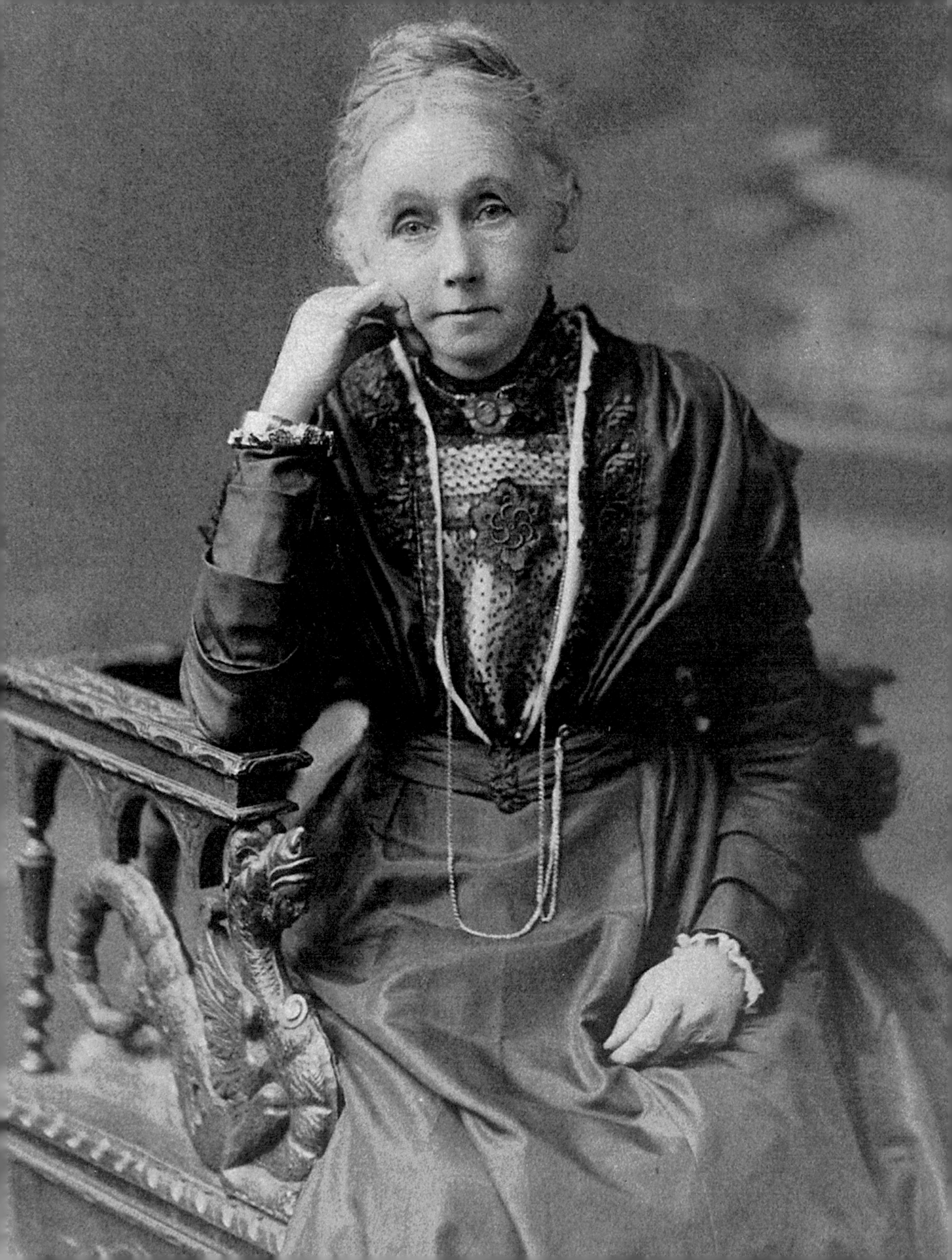

This photograph shows the rear of Susannah Place with the 'Cheap Cash Grocer' sign of No 64 Gloucester Street (shop). It is one of a series of photographs commissioned after the outbreak of bubonic plague in The Rocks. In contrast to posed studio photographs, this 1901 photo captures people dressed in their everyday clothes with hair out of place, children with bare feet and women with their sleeves rolled up.

Cumberland Place towards Whalers Arms Hotel, Government Printing Office, glass negative, 1901, State Records NSW

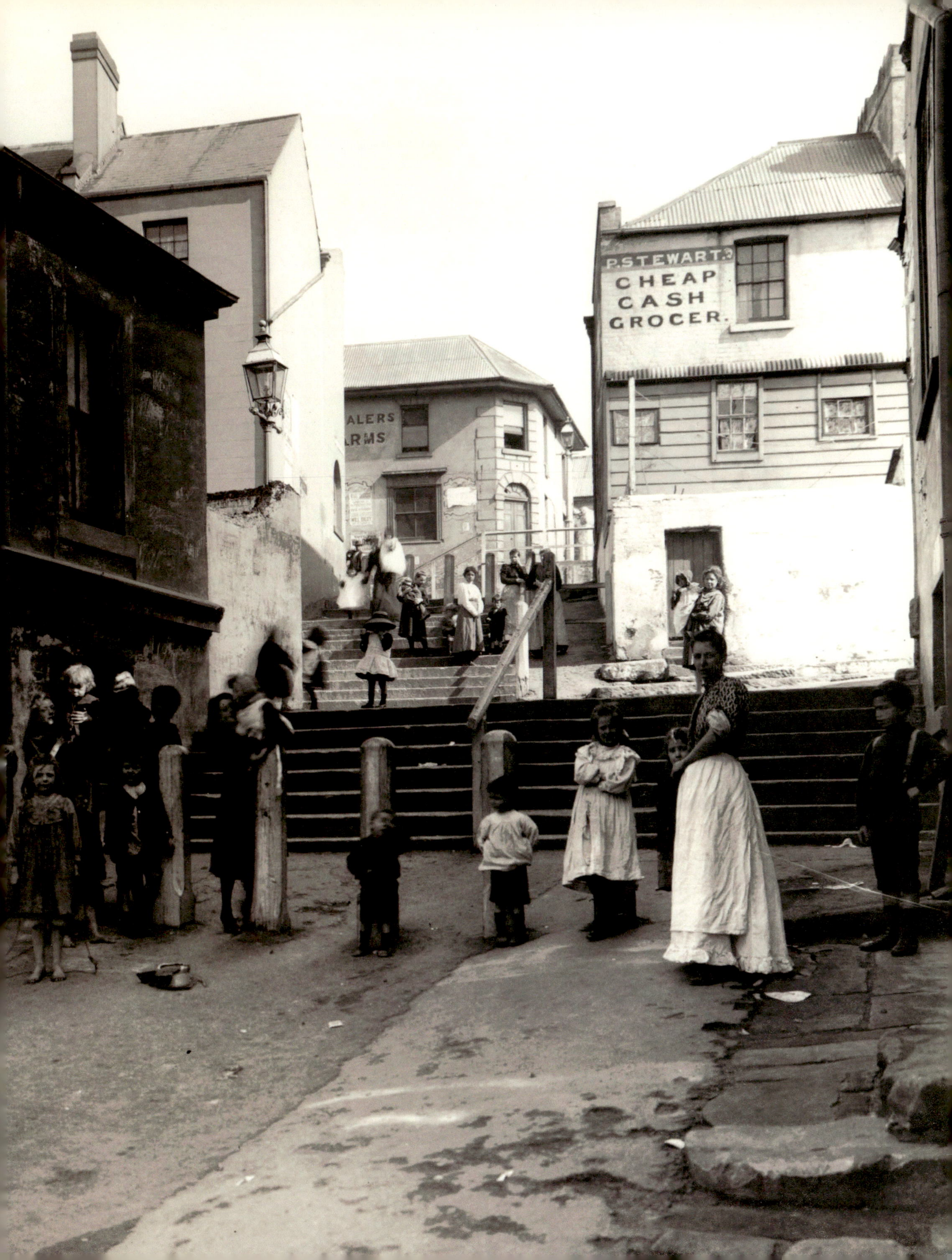
P. STEWART
CHEAP
CASH
GROCER.
ALERS
ARMS

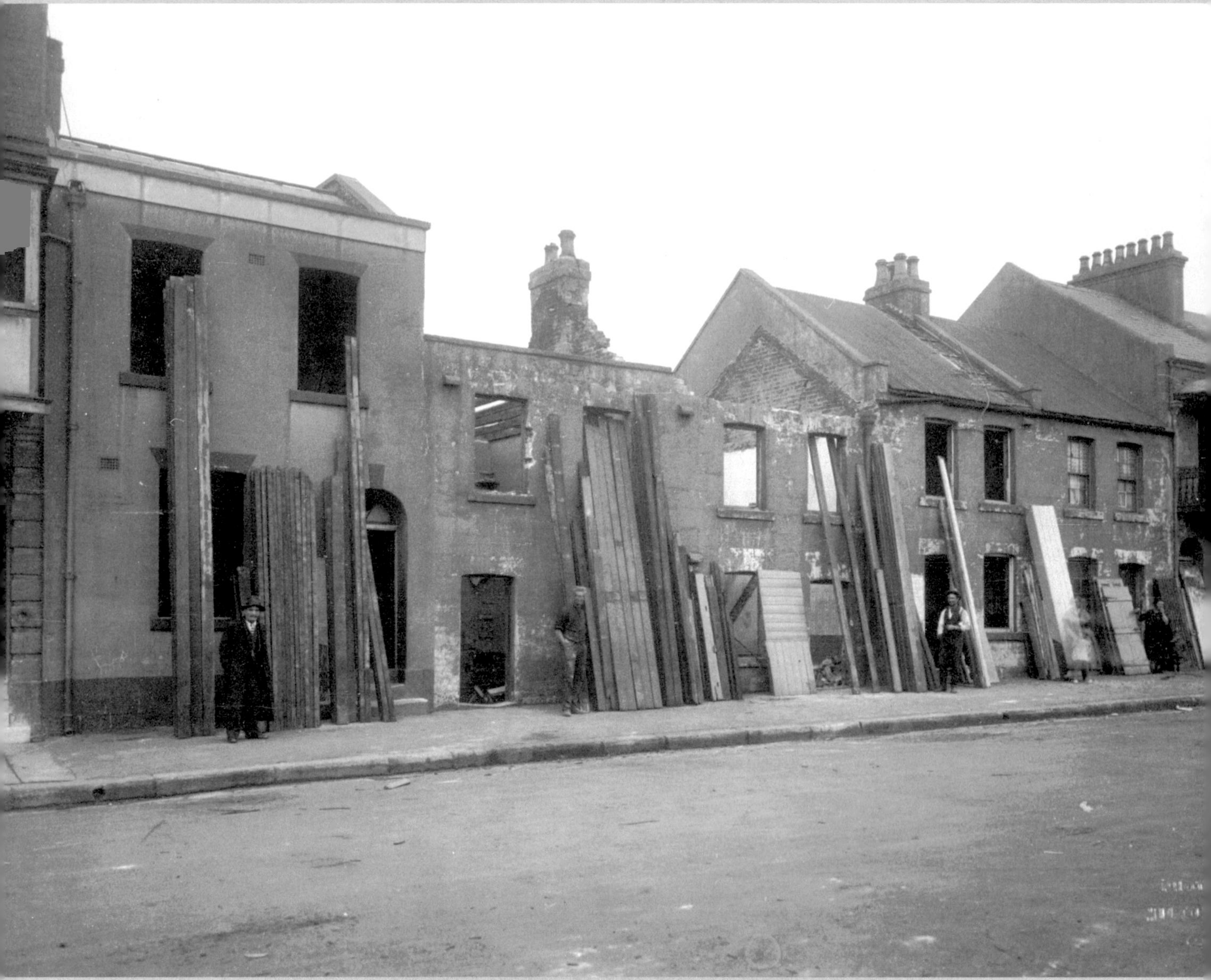

Only the sandstone bones of the land remain. The hills have become slighter in grade, the gullies filled, the sea driven back, a forest of steel and concrete cacti has sprung from the rind of the earth.[30]

Ruth Park, 1973

By the 1930s the whole of Princes Street had been demolished to build the approaches to the Sydney Harbour Bridge, and many people began to lament the disappearance of 'Old Sydney' as the area was affectionately called. A 1932 article declared The Rocks the 'Cradle of Sydney', recalling the

> Small but stoutly-built cottages [that] stood alongside more pretentious houses, the poor among the rich in a riot of architectural vagaries, which added materially to their attractiveness.[31]

The area we call The Rocks today was created in 1970 with the formation of the Sydney Cove Redevelopment Authority (SCRA). In contrast to the 24 hectares managed by the SCRA – from the southern approach to the Harbour Bridge to Grosvenor Street and the foreshore of the western side of Sydney Cove[32] – The Rocks of the 19th century covered a much smaller area from Argyle Street to Charlotte Place (now Grosvenor Street). Eliza Walker recalled that in the 1840s 'The Rocks' referred specifically to the streets behind 'Gallows Hill' (Harrington Street – its original name was because of the view it gave of the hangings at George Street gaol) where it was 'built all over with small houses and cottages for the working people, such as seamen and wharf labourers'.[33]

With the high-rise expansion of the city and the redevelopment of The Rocks in the 1970s the southern side of the Cahill Expressway became a sacrificial zone. As the SCRA explained, 'Income obtained from leasing vacant land to the south ... will pay for the restoration and upkeep of historic buildings'.[34]

Today, The Rocks is a tourist precinct, with high-class shops and restaurants in restored warehouses and houses. There

56–62 Princes Street, The Rocks (prior to demolition for the construction of the Harbour Bridge), 18 July 1927, glass plate negative, City of Sydney Archives

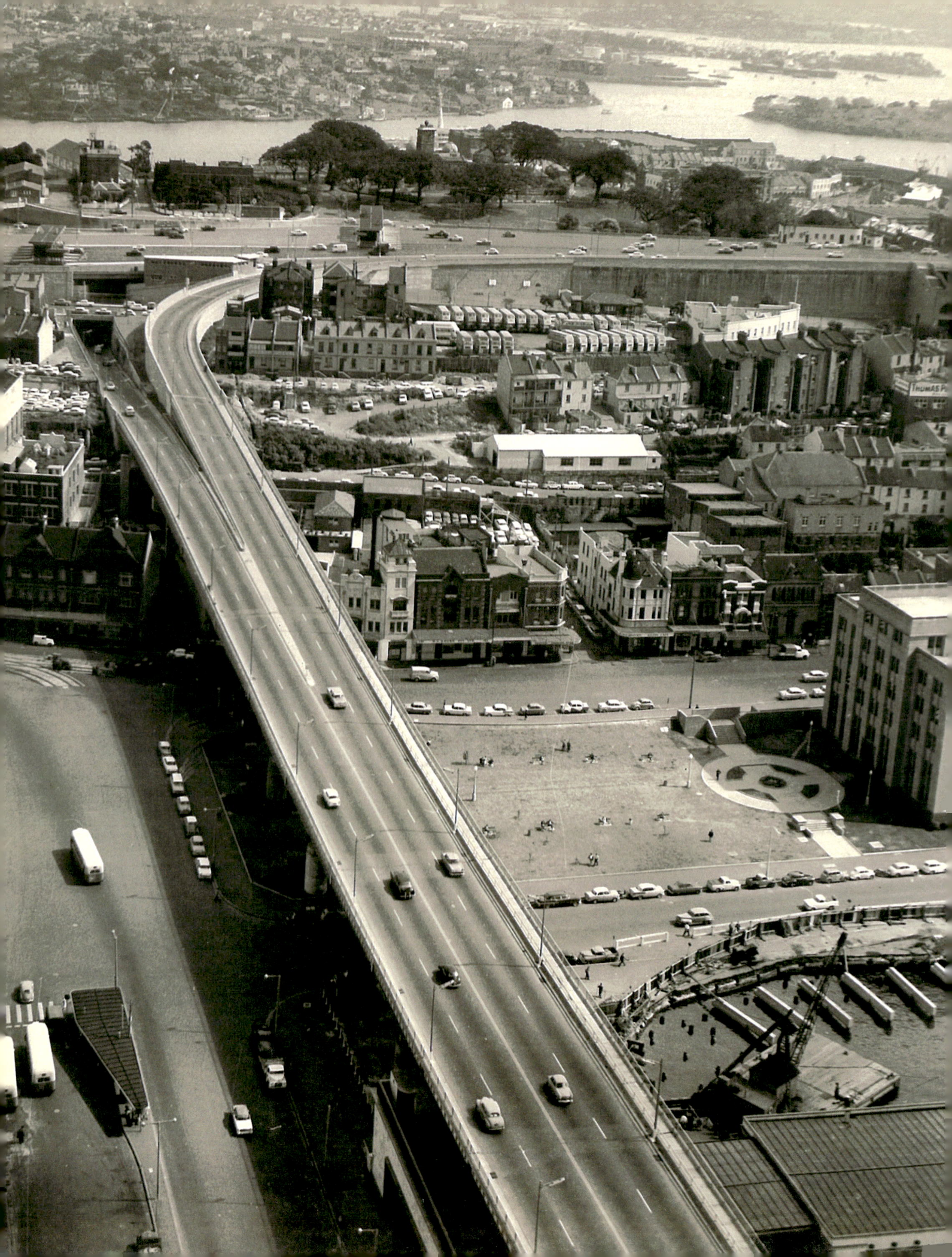

The powerful forces of commerce are held back from the harbour by that bland concrete motorway — the Cahill Expressway.[35]

Sydney Architecture Walks, 2007

The Rocks, on the right of the Cahill Expressway. Susannah Place is above and to the right of the large white shed. Aerial view of Cahill Expressway at Circular Quay, 9 April 1962, City of Sydney Archives

are still a lot of hotels but now they serve city workers and international tourists. The historic buildings that survived the succession of demolitions are now protected and admired. Working-class residents retain a presence thanks to the Department of Housing and to the threads of memory and artefacts that generations have left behind. As historian and archaeologist Grace Karskens said of the archaeological site at Cumberland and Gloucester streets:

> *If we could map these houses, not just as anonymous walls and floors, but in terms of the relationships of the people who lived in them over time, the map would be like an impossibly complex web, with hundreds of interwoven threads.*[36]

This is a fitting description for the whole of The Rocks. People were forever moving in and out of houses – across the road, around the corner or to the street below. Many families lived in the area for generations but others stayed only a few years before moving on. Connections abounded: families were related through marriage, children attended school together, men worked alongside each other on the wharfs – all the while witnessing each other's marriages and lending each other money. Shirly Andersen recalls that her husband, Jack, who had been born and raised in The Rocks, 'would have given his eye teeth to get back there' in later years.[37] In 1956 Ellen and Dennis Marshall came to a boarding house at 109 Gloucester Street for what they thought would be a short stay in the area:

> *We came to see about the room and Mrs Stigg said, 'Don't take it', and I said 'why?' and she said, 'because if you take the room you'll never leave The Rocks'. I said, 'Oh six weeks at the most for me here ... it will only be until we get something else'.*[38]

Ellen and her husband remained in The Rocks for 34 years. For 28 of those years they lived at 62 Gloucester Street, which to this day Ellen refers to as 'home'.

Did we realise how unique it was? We knew it was old, thought it was beaut, left with regret; knowing too late, that no place, ever again, would be quite like The Rocks.[39]

Cedric Flower, 1969

WORDS ON THE ROCKS

Panorama Sydney Harbour and Circular Quay (detail), Melvin Vaniman, hand-coloured photograph, 1907, Sydney Harbour Foreshore Authority

top left [West Circular Quay, Sydney] [c1875–85] albumen photoprint, Small Picture File collection, Mitchell Library, State Library of New South Wales **top right** Circular Quay [west], c1900–10, albumen photoprint, Mitchell Library, State Library of New South Wales **bottom left** Circular Quay, Sydney, 1877, albumen photoprint, Small Picture File collection, Mitchell Library, State Library of New South Wales **bottom right** Circular Quay, 1873, Holtermann Collection, Mitchell Library, State Library of New South Wales

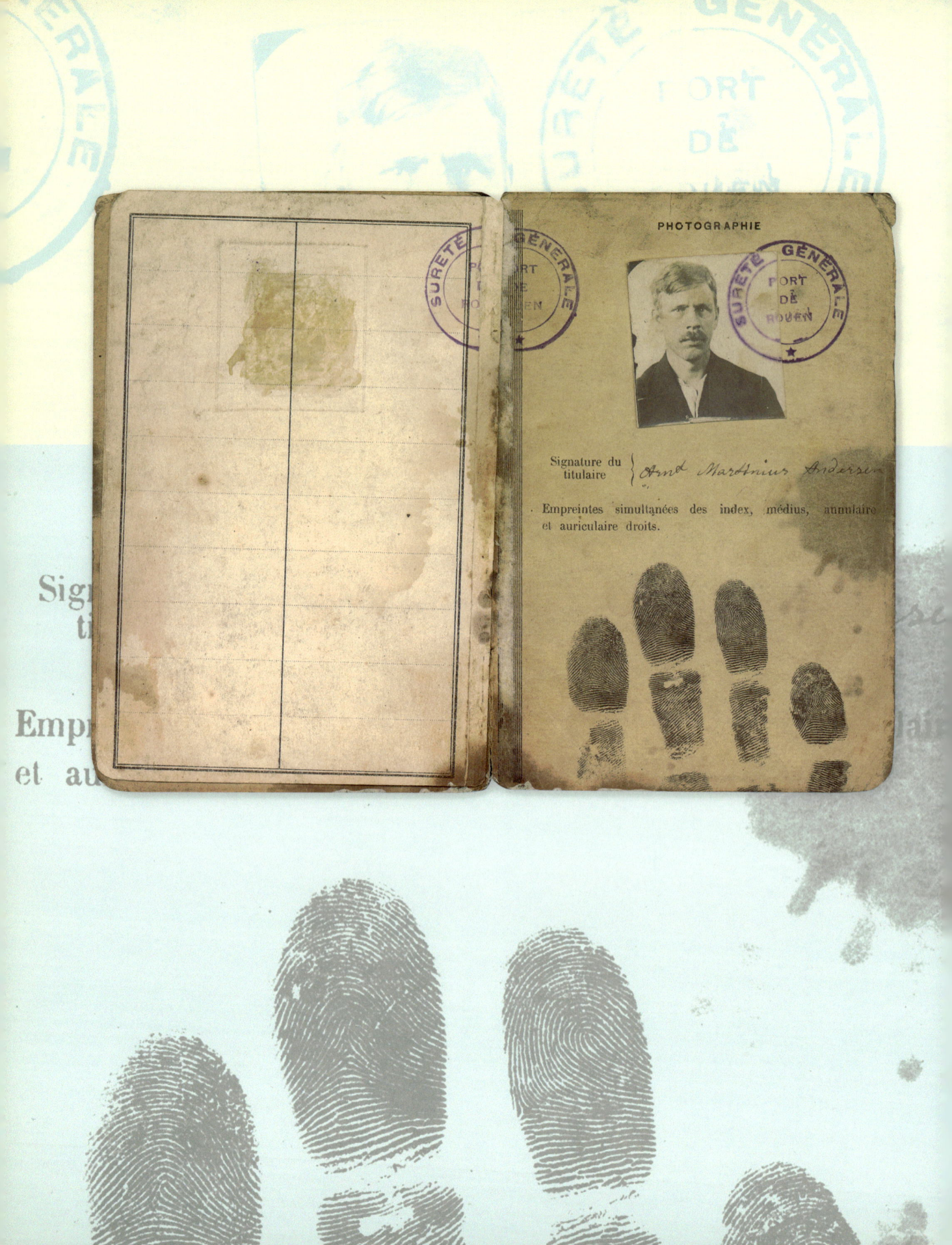

PHOTOGRAPHIE

Signature du titulaire { Arnt Martinius Andersen

Empreintes simultanées des index, médius, annulaire et auriculaire droits.

Arnt Martinius Andersen (known as Martin) is listed as a sailor on his identity papers. Martin was originally from Kristiania (now Oslo), Norway, and the document records the ports he travelled to while working on board a Norwegian ship from 1918 to 1919. As well as a photograph and fingerprints the document records his physical description, including a tattoo that read 'in memory of my dear mother'. It is unknown when Martin came to Australia but in 1927, aged 38, he married local Rocks woman Mary Pauline Gallagher and they had two sons. Martin worked as a ship's carpenter at Garden Island until his retirement in the early 1950s.

Identity document of Arnt Martinius Andersen, 1918. Tenant No 64 Gloucester Street, 1937–49 and No 58 Gloucester Street, 1949–63. Courtesy Terri Williams

WORDS ON THE ROCKS

1. William C Wentworth, *Statistical, historical and political description of the Colony of New South Wales and its dependent settlements in Van Diemen's Land*, facsimile reprint, Griffin Press Limited, Adelaide, 1978, p7 (first published G & W B Whittaker, London, 1819).
2. Peter Cunningham, *Two years in New South Wales: a series of letters, comprising sketches of the actual state of that colony, of its peculiar advantages to emigrants, of its topography, natural history*, David S Macmillan (ed), Angus & Robertson, Sydney, 1966, p29 (first published in 1827).
3. Reverend Johnson quoted in Dr John Cobley (ed), *Sydney Cove 1788: the first year of the settlement of Australia*, Hodder & Stoughton, London, 1962, p255.
4. J T Bigge, *Report of the Commissioner of Inquiry, on the state of agriculture and trade in the Colony of New South Wales*, London, 1823, Australiana Facsimile Editions No 70, Libraries Board of South Australia, Adelaide, 1966, p42.
5. J T Bigge, *Report of the Commissioner of Inquiry, on the judicial establishments of New South Wales, and Van Diemen's Land*, London, 1823, Australiana Facsimile Editions No 60, Libraries Board of South Australia, Adelaide, 1966, p62.
6. Lieutenant King quoted in Cobley (ed), *Sydney Cove 1788*, p38.
7. *Sydney Gazette*, 6 October 1810.
8. *Sydney Gazette*, 8 December 1805.
9. *Sydney Gazette*, 26 June 1803.
10. Barani – Indigenous History of Sydney City website, viewed June 2007, <http://www.cityofsydney.nsw.gov.au/barani>.
11. Cobley (ed), *Sydney Cove 1788*, p31.
12. Eliza Walker & S K Johnstone, 'Old Sydney in the 'forties: recollections of Lower George Street and "The Rocks"', *Journal of the Royal Australian Historical Society*, vol 16, 1930, p310.
13. Surgeon John White, *Journal of a voyage to New South Wales*, J Debrett, London, 1790, journal entry 26 January 1788.
14. Robert A Moore, *Conservation analysis and guidelines: Susannah Place*, 1989, unpublished, p8.
15. Fred Hughes oral history, 1992.
16. Alexander Harris, *Settlers and convicts: or recollections of sixteen years' hard labour in the Australian backwoods*, Melbourne University Press, Melbourne, 1953, p10 (first published in London, 1847).
17. William Stanley Jevons, 'Remarks upon the social map of Sydney, 1858', manuscript, Microfilm CY 1045, Mitchell Library, State Library of New South Wales, p22.
18. Wendy Thorp, *Report of the excavations at Lilyvale* (draft), unpublished report, prepared for CRI Pty Ltd, 1994.
19. ibid
20. A J C Mayne, *Fever, squalor and vice: sanitation and social policy in Victorian Sydney*, University of Queensland Press, St Lucia, 1982, Appendix 1.
21. *Sydney Morning Herald*, 1 January 1851 to 15 March 1851.
22. Select Committee on the Condition of the Working Classes of the Metropolis, Minutes of evidence, *Votes and Proceedings of the Legislative Assembly of New South Wales*, 1859–60, vol 4, p169.
23. Eliza Walker, 'Old Sydney in the 'forties', pp298 and 309.

left Laundry wall, No 58 Gloucester Street (detail), 2004, photograph © Ross Heathcote **centre** Clara Youngein, c1915. Tenant No 64 Gloucester Street, 1904–17. Courtesy Young family **right** Front door, No 60 Gloucester Street, 2004, photograph © Ross Heathcote

24 'The tragedy of "The Rocks": a peep into Sydney's slum area', *Building*, 12 November 1913, p90.
25 ibid
26 A J C Mayne, *Fever, squalor and vice*, p103.
27 Peter Emmett, *Sydney: metropolis, suburb, harbour*, Historic Houses Trust, Sydney, 2000, p43.
28 Fred Hughes oral history, 1992; Fred Hughes and Bertha Grayson (nee Hughes) oral history, 1994.
29 Fred Hughes and Bertha Grayson oral history, 1994.
30 Ruth Park, *A companion guide to Sydney*, Collins, Sydney, 1973, p15.
31 Colin Harrison, 'It was the cradle of Sydney', *Daily Telegraph*, 19 March 1932, p17.
32 Noni Boyd, 'Gloucester Street, The Rocks (from the Argyle Cut to the Cahill Expressway): a study of its development and conservation', unpublished thesis, 1997.
33 Eliza Walker, 'Old Sydney in the 'forties', p303.
34 *Welcome to The Rocks*, [pamphlet] undated, Sydney Cove Redevelopment Authority.
35 Sydney Architecture Walks, viewed November 2006, <http://www.sydneyarchitecture.org>.
36 Grace Karskens, *Inside the Rocks: the archaeology of a neighbourhood*, Hale & Iremonger, Sydney, 1999, p168.
37 Jack and Shirly Andersen oral history, 1992.
38 Ellen Marshall oral history, 1992.
39 Cedric Flower and John Carnemolla, *The Rocks*, Horwitz, Sydney, 1969, Introduction.

left Exterior southern wall, No 64 Gloucester Street (detail), 2004, photograph © Ross Heathcote **centre** Girlie Andersen (second from left), c1940s. Tenant No 58 Gloucester Street, 1949–64. Courtesy Terri Williams **right** Air vent, No 58 Gloucester Street (detail), 2004, photograph © Ross Heathcote

Sydney Town in lime-wash and soft brick effaced the tents and palm logs of Phillip's settlement; the sandstone palaces of the 19th century boom town dwarfed these little survivors; the glittering steel on glass towers laughed at the grimy Victoriana.[1]

Peter Tonkin, 2000

FROM THE

2

GROUND UP

A capital and substantial dwelling House, With Attic story, Kitchen and wash-house, and good Garden, containing three Lemon Trees, two Orange ditto, a number of early Newington Peach-trees, and a capital Well …[2]

Sydney Gazette, 1803

In November 1788, ten months after the European settlement of Australia, a female convict described the shaky beginnings of the town of Sydney:

> We now have two streets, if four of the most miserable huts you can possibly conceive of deserve that name. Windows they have none, as from the Governor's house, &c., now nearly finished, no glass could be spared; so that lattices of twigs are made by our people to supply their places.[3]

The 'our people' referred to are the convicts who built their huts on the rocky ledges on the western side of Sydney Cove from the trees and scrubs found growing in the local area. These early huts proved no match for the heavy rains and strong winds that beset the infant colony. Over the next 30 years more substantial houses began to appear 'on the rocks', though the majority were still timber with thatched or shingled roofs. In the 1820s Commissioner Bigge counted in Sydney 59 stone houses, 221 brick houses, and 773 built of timber, belonging to private individuals.[4]

In 1827 Surgeon Cunningham described the 'rows rising above rows of neat white cottages'[5] and two years later, newly arrived surveyor Felton Mathew found a more established town with 'some pretty cottages' where the 'so called "streets" resemble the suburbs of London, small houses with little strips of garden in front, some in rows, some detached'.[6]

Up until the 1830s many people simply claimed land in The Rocks as their own and, without any official grant, proceeded to build houses on it. An 1823 report estimated that 'four-fifths' of the houses in Sydney were claimed by 'permissive occupancy'.[7] Despite this lack of legal ownership, houses and land were on-sold numerous times, and by the 1830s, when Governor Darling began the process of

West view of Sydney-Cove taken from the Rocks, at the rear of the General Hospital, not signed or dated, pen ink and wash on wove paper, Dixson Galleries, State Library of New South Wales **previous page** *View of Sydney, From the West side of the Cove*. No. 2 (detail), John Eyre, 1810, hand coloured aquatint, Mitchell Library, State Library of New South Wales

37

The Latter the Property of
Edwd. Macarthur, Esqre,
Divided into Allotments
for Building.
1836.

Note: The part tinted Brown shews the ground reclaimable from the
Green, is proposed to be reserved.
Yellow, shews what is proposed as a reserve for Fortification.
Pink, as a site for a Church.
Blue, is reserved for a Wharf.

	a. r. p.
Pyrmont contains	60.1.16
Reserved	13.1.0
do for Church	1.0.32
do Fortification	1.2.0
do Wharf	1.0.0
Reclaimable Land, about	10.0.0

The Allotments from 1 to 48, are one Chain in width, three in depth, and contain three squa[re]
From 49 to 79 they are one Chain wide & of different depths. From 80 to 86 they are two Chains in
frontage & of various depths. From 87 to 99 they are of irregular dimensions & contents

N.B. The Soundings are in F[eet]

granting freehold title, much of the land in The Rocks was found to have already been 'owned' for 40 or more years. This led to a flood of people trying to prove their ownership through memorials to the Commissioner of Claims, some of which took years to untangle, especially in cases involving multiple claims. Reading through these memorials today reveals the history not only of a particular piece of land, but of the complex financial dealings between individuals that sometimes spanned generations.

The land occupied by Susannah Place today, bound to the east by Cambridge Street and to the west by Gloucester Street, has just such a history of convoluted claims and counterclaims going back to 1816 when two men, William Walsh and Dennis Conway, each owned a building on the site. Conway had come to the colony as a convict in 1797 and Walsh had arrived as a free man with his convict wife in 1810. It is not known how the two men met but within a few years of Walsh's arrival they lived side by side in adjoining houses. In 1815 the enterprising Walsh acquired a publican's licence and the 'memorials' allude to an inn called the Duke of Wellington operating on the site. At the time it was not unusual for people to convert a room in their house and sell spirits. Not long afterwards, Walsh succeeded in securing an indenture in which Dennis Conway 'did assign bargain transfer and make over to the said William Walsh ... all that dwelling house situate lying and being No 6 Gloucester Street Sydney'.[8] According to a witness, Mr Rampling, Walsh 'had always a desire to get the premises from Conway' and 'Walsh took advantage of Conway being drunk and got him to sign the deed'. Mr Rampling further declared, 'Conway had been made drunk' for this very purpose.[9]

Auction sale Observatory Hill Lands [cartographic material]: Plan no. 3, Department of Lands, 4 December 1905, Mitchell Library, State Library of New South Wales **opposite** *Plan of Sydney with Pyrmont, New South Wales: the latter of the property of Edw. Macarthur Esquire, divided into allotments for building*, 1836, J Basire, Mitchell Library, State Library of New South Wales

In May 1834, long after the deaths of Walsh and Conway, Conway's grandson, John Norman, disputed William Walsh Junior's ownership of the site. After gathering evidence from witnesses recalling the events of 15 years earlier, the Commissioner of Claims found in favour of Norman. Ironically, not long after the claim was settled, Walsh Junior's widow, Harriet, purchased the site from Norman. But Harriet's venture was short-lived; by December 1835 her financial difficulties were such that the sheriff forced her to sell the property. The land and buildings were bought for £220 by an ex-convict, James Byrne, who also owned the well patronised hotel, the St Patrick's Inn (later renamed the Whalers Arms), directly across the road.

It was not until 1836 that Byrne's ownership was legitimised by way of a Town Grant for which he was required to pay a yearly quit rent of ten shillings until 1849, and from then on five shillings on condition that within two years he build a 'permanent dwelling house, store or other suitable building ... and shall construct proper drains from the same land, to the nearest common drain or sewer'.[10] These conditions were part of the government's attempt to rid the town of poorly built or dilapidated structures and were followed in 1837 with the introduction of new building regulations.

After Byrne's death in 1838 the property passed to his wife Sarah. It appears she also inherited substantial debts, or perhaps spent her inheritance unwisely, for in 1842 she was forced to sell by public auction most of the property she had acquired, including St Patrick's Inn and the Gloucester Street site containing Walsh's and Conway's old homes:

VALUABLE HOUSE PROPERTY
IN SYDNEY LOT I
Contains freehold premises, consisting of a six-roomed cottage, and appurtenances, situate in and being the corner house of Cambridge-street and Gloucester-street, in Sydney ... at a rental of one pound per week; and the three-room Cottage, yard and appurtenances, adjoining the last mentioned Cottage ... at a rental of sixteen shillings per week.[11]

The same year that James Byrne died saw the arrival in the colony of assisted Irish immigrants Edward and Mary Riley and Mary's daughter, Susannah Sterne. Their entitlement certificates list Edward as a farmer, Mary as a nursery governess and Susannah as a milliner, and records them

This photograph was taken a few years before Gloucester Street was raised. The Youngein grocer shop has a striped curtain hanging over the window. Gloucester Street near Cumberland Place, 15 Oct 1910, albumen photoprint, Mitchell Library, State Library of New South Wales

Gloucester St., near Cumberland Pl
15 Oct. 1910

42

FROM THE GROUND UP

Working parties of chain-ganged convicts in yellow and grey came down each morning from Hyde Park Barracks ... to do their patient picking ...[12]

Isadore Brodsky, 1962

Numerous merchants agitated for a short cut between the busy waterfronts of Sydney Cove and Darling Harbour. In 1843, using convict labour, work began on cutting through the solid sandstone ridge that divided The Rocks and Millers Point. This work using simple tools was very slow despite the harsh supervision of overseer Timothy Lane, whose cry was 'with the help of God and the strong arm of the flogger, you'll get fifty before breakfast tomorrow'.[13] The newly formed Sydney Municipal Council eventually completed the Argyle Cut in 1859 using explosives and paid labour. In the 1860s a series of bridges were built to reconnect the streets that had been severed by the cutting. Stone excavated from the cutting was used to construct the sea wall at Circular Quay.

Argyle Cut, Harold Cazneaux, 1912, gelatin silver photograph, National Gallery of Australia

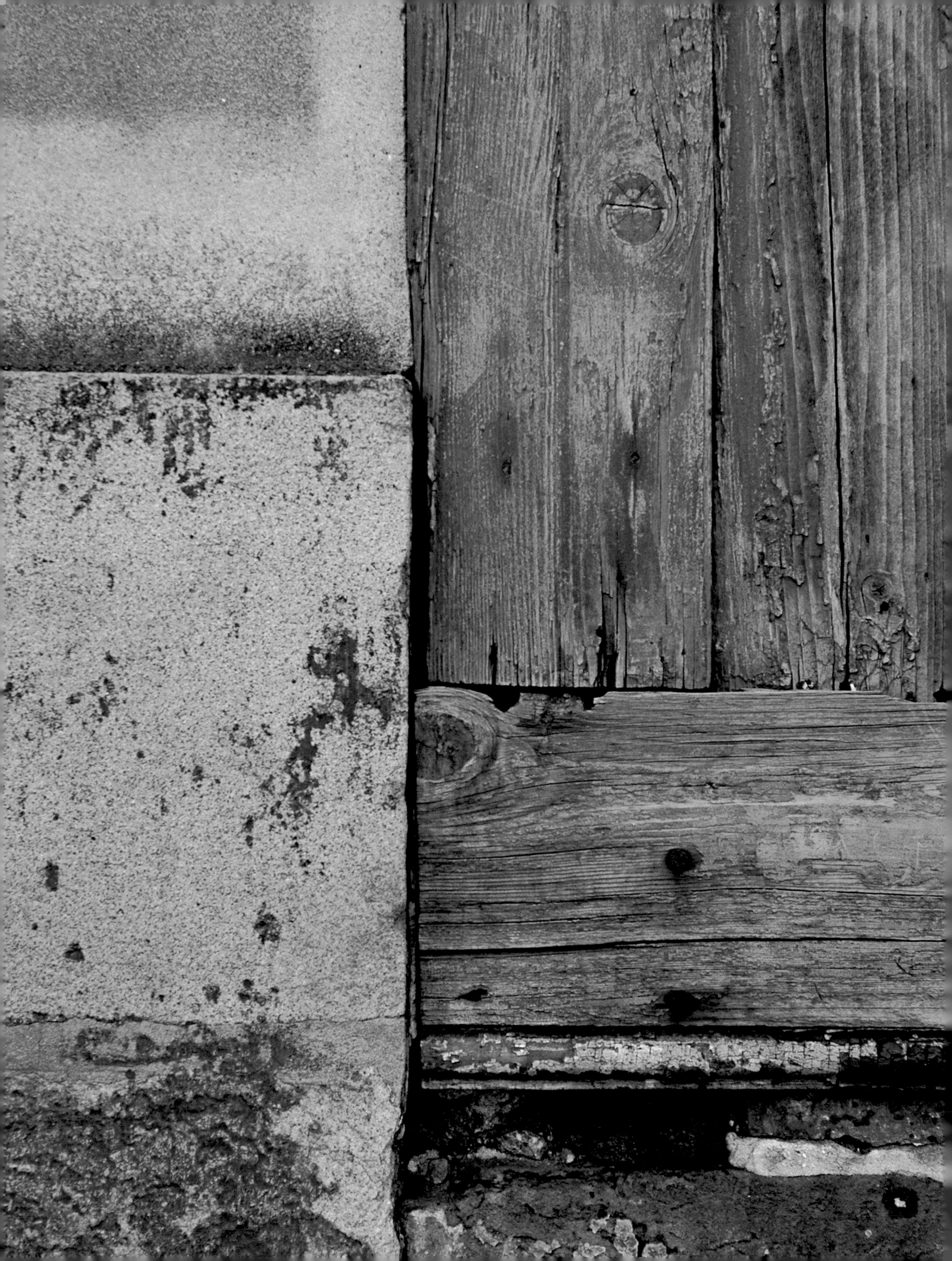

FROM THE GROUND UP

> *Decidedly, the surest way for a capitalist ... to invest his capital ... is to erect houses of cheap and useful description ... such as may accommodate small families and individuals of the middling, mercantile, and working classes of the community.*[14]

Reverend Henry Carmichael, 1834

all as being able to read and write.[15] It is still a mystery how after only four years in the colony, and despite the depression of the 1840s, the Rileys had accumulated the capital to purchase the Byrnes' 'valuable' property for the considerable sum of £450.

The Rileys invested in The Rocks at an opportune time. In 1842, with a population of nearly 30,000 people, the town of Sydney was declared a city. Being a city of walking scale with limited public transportation, accommodation in The Rocks became highly desirable for its convenient central location and proximity to work. Such was the demand that a two-room house described as 'in bad repair no outhouses' still commanded a yearly rent of £15.[16]

Exploiting the market, many large allotments and gardens established in the early years of the colony were subdivided and multiple dwellings with little or no gardens were crammed onto ever-diminishing plots of land. Within two years of their purchase the Rileys had demolished the existing six- and three-room cottages and built in their place a terrace of four houses described as 'new with basement kitchens'.[17] The terrace was named, not in the usual fashion after its owner, but after Riley's stepdaughter, Susannah Sterne, even though she never

Susannah Place plaque, 1991, photograph © Christopher Shain **opposite** Southern wall, No 64 Gloucester Street (detail), 2004, photograph © Ross Heathcote

FROM THE GROUND UP

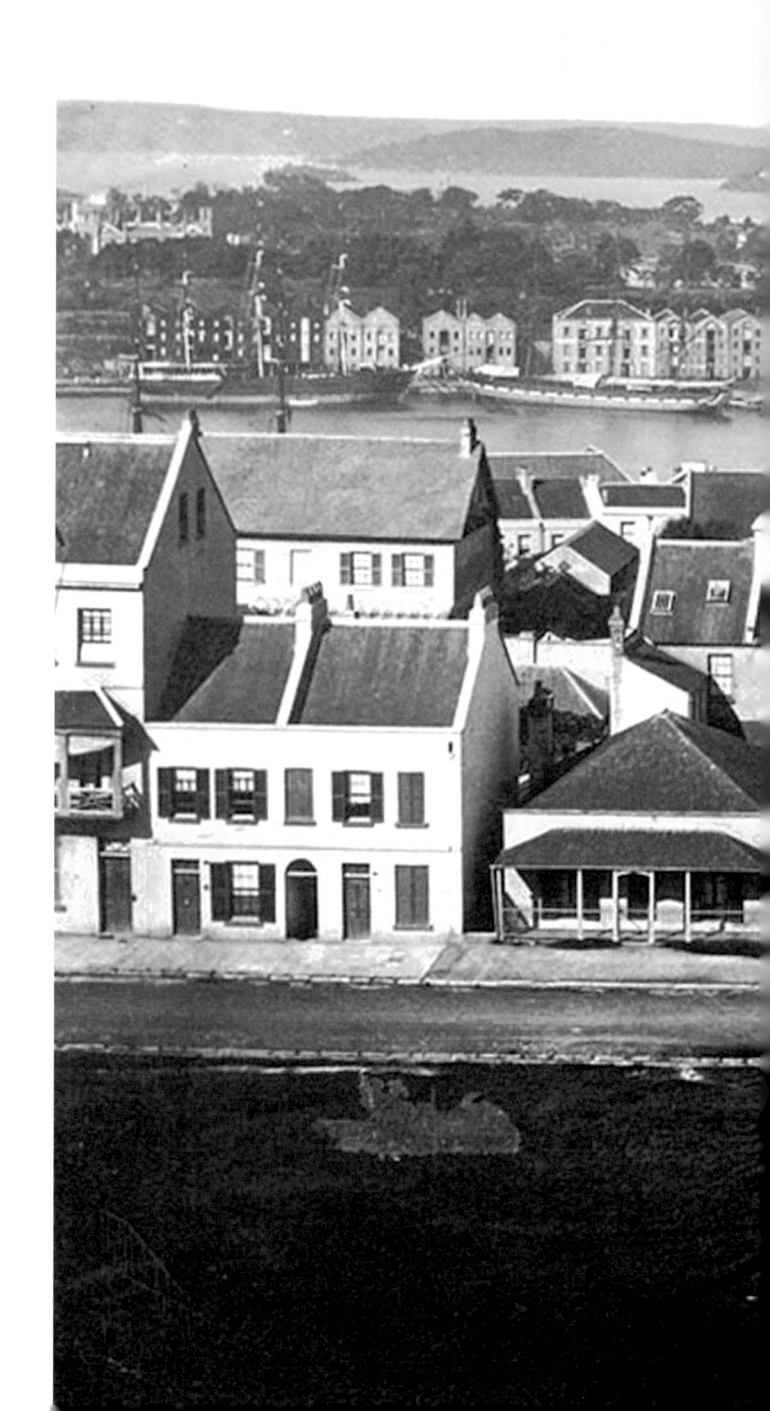

Sydney Cove from Flagstaff [Hill], c1873, albumen photoprint, Small Picture File collection, Mitchell Library, State Library of New South Wales

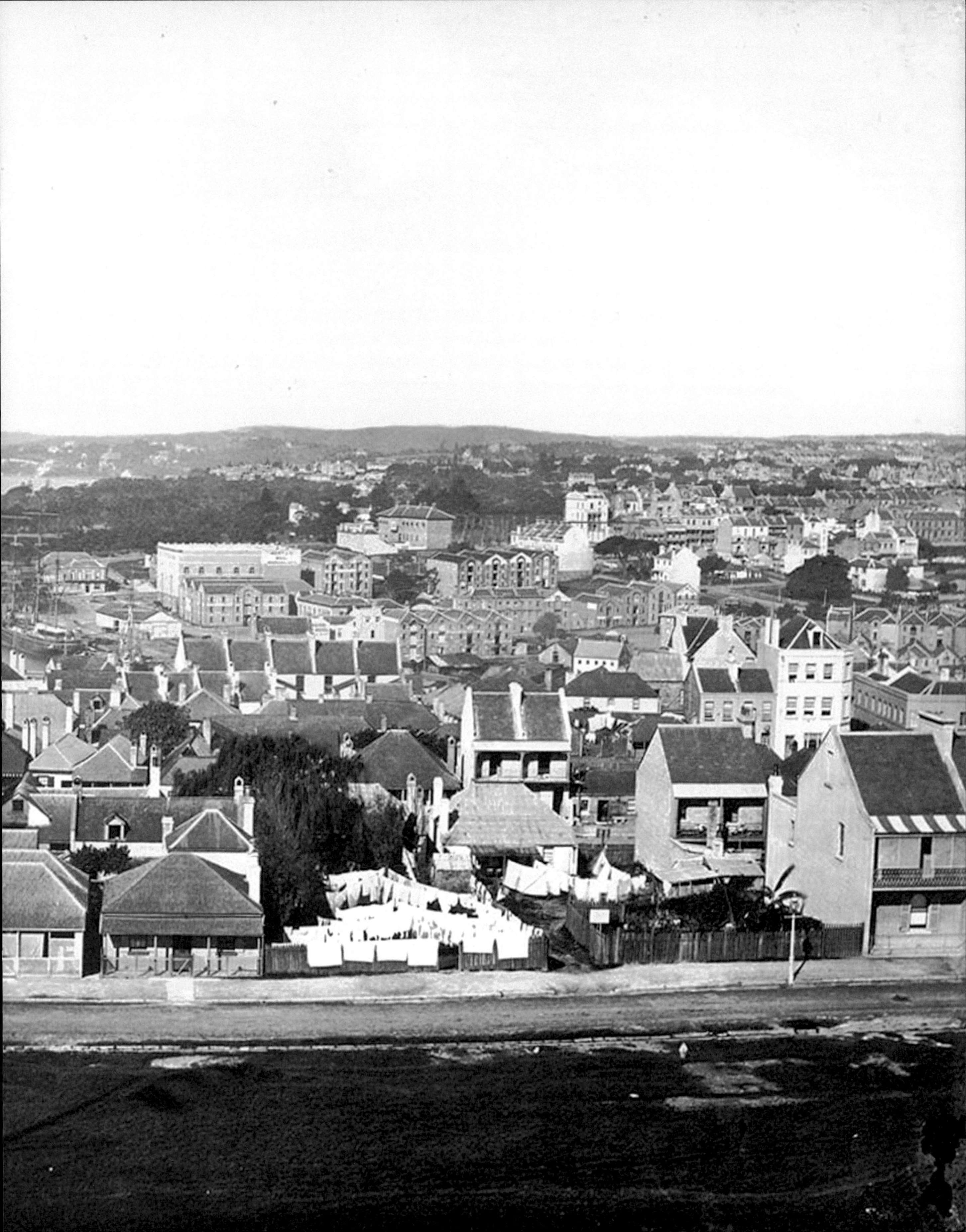

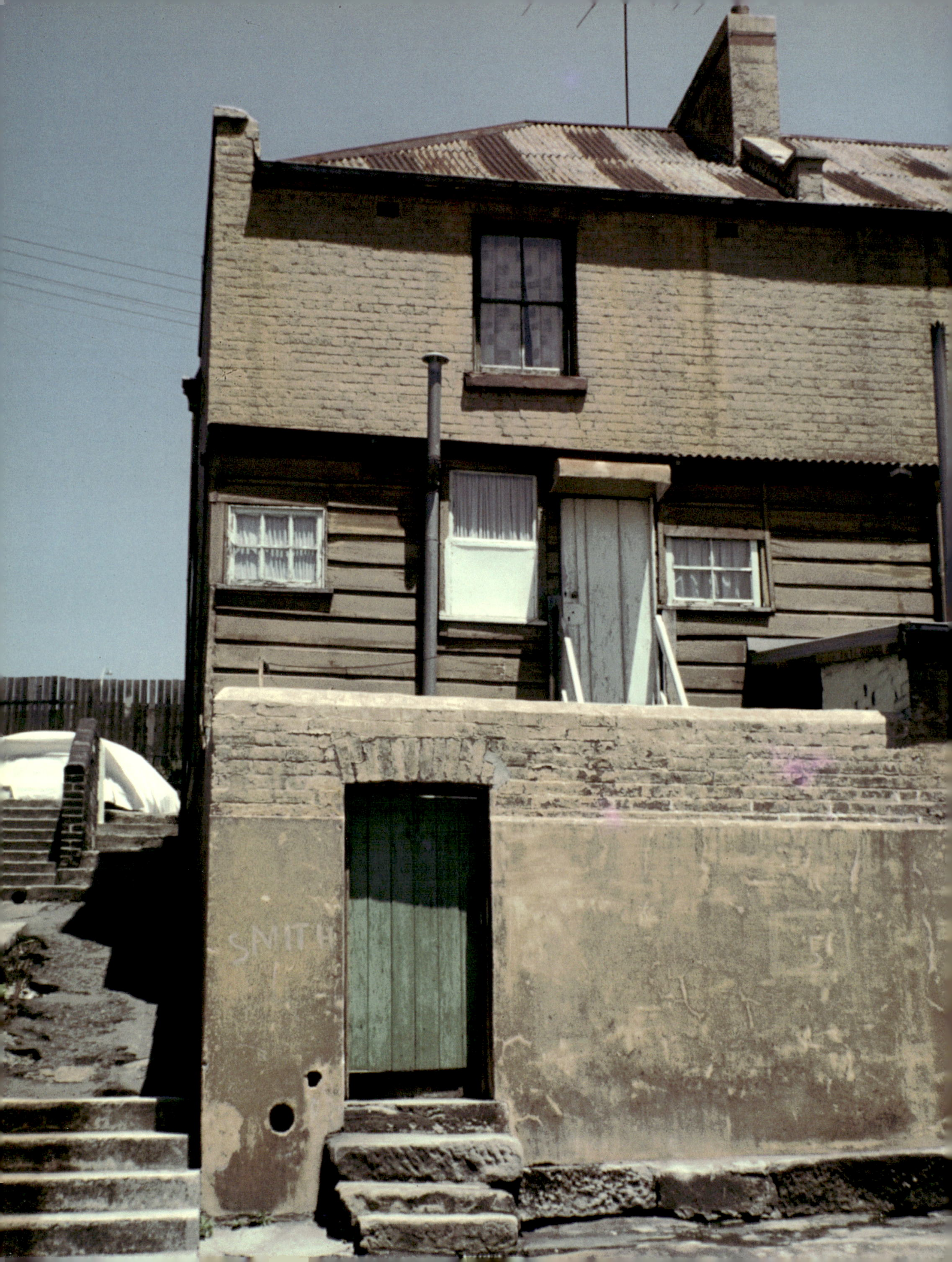
SMITH

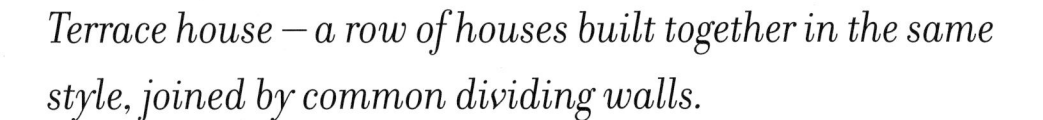

Terrace house – a row of houses built together in the same style, joined by common dividing walls.

lived at the property. On the facade a sandstone plaque, still visible today, reads 'Susannah Place Anno Domini 1844'.

The builders of Susannah Place followed the English designs known to them. The result was a typically English terrace transplanted to a new environment. The houses followed the 'basic plan' of English terrace housing: two floors with two rooms each and included the common variation of a basement.[18]

Susannah Place was built on the sandstone ridge of Gloucester Street. This sloping site allowed for the inclusion of a basement kitchen and cellar, which were partially cut into the bedrock. The houses thus appear to be three storeys when viewed from behind in Cambridge Street. Photographs of Cambridge Street in the early 20th century (see pages 52–53, for example) show houses perched further along the sandstone ledge, but unlike those houses, which looked to the harbour, Susannah Place faced Gloucester Street.

The houses were built of colonial bond brickwork with a shingled roof. The corner house included a shop in the front room with a splayed corner entrance and large windows facing Gloucester Street and Cumberland Place designed to attract passing trade. From 1890 the four houses that constitute Susannah Place were numbered 58 to 64 Gloucester Street, by which they continue to be known today.

In her memoirs Eliza Walker recalls a public fountain that was located to the south of Susannah Place in Long's Lane:

Further along Gloucester Street, we came to the pump from which the people got their supply of water for domestic use. Some of the residents had wells, but these from time to time became dry.[19]

By the 1840s many of the wells described in Eliza's memoirs were no longer in use as a result of contamination from years of poor drainage that 'simply trickle[d] down the hill, soon reaching ... the front and back of the next lower house'.[20] In 1859 The Select Committee on the Condition of the Working Classes, reporting on the conditions in Long's Lane, noted that

Rear, No 64 Gloucester Street, photograph Alan Mitchell Stuthridge, c1958–1970, Caroline Simpson Library & Research Collection, Historic Houses Trust

P. STEWART?
CHEAP
CASH
GROCER.

there was only one water tap to seven houses and the water-closets built near the back doors created a 'very offensive' smell.[21] A pawnbroker giving evidence to the Select Committee described his neighbours in The Rocks: 'Just near where I am living there are nine small houses and only one small closet, with no drainage'. When asked how such conditions affected the health of the local children he stated, 'my children have suffered. I have buried one from it'.[22]

In stark contrast, the tenants of Susannah Place enjoyed far better facilities. By 1855 the houses had been connected to the water supply and by 1860 each house had been connected to the sewer, which drained into Sydney Cove. The reason for Susannah Place's superior plumbing may lie in the fact that unlike many absentee landlords, the Rileys lived in one of the houses, providing a constant presence for 30 years.

The death of Mary Riley in 1874 brought a change of ownership. Mary's house and the adjacent corner shop (Nos 62 and 64) were left to her granddaughter, Mary Anne Finnigan, while the other two houses (Nos 58 and 60) were left for the 'benefit of the Church or School in the Parishes of St Philip's and the Holy Trinity Sydney'.[23]

The ownership of Susannah Place did not change again until 1901 when the state government resumed The Rocks following the outbreak of bubonic plague in Sydney. From then on the houses were owned and administered by successive government authorities, although for most tenants life went on as normal.

Mary Anne Finnigan (nee Hensley), c1900. Owner Nos 62 and 64 Gloucester Street, 1874–1901. Courtesy Willis family **opposite** Rear of Susannah Place terrace, Cumberland Place, The Rocks, Mitchell Library, State Library of New South Wales

Houses perched along the sandstone ridge in Cambridge Street. [Photographs of] Buildings condemned and pulled down. [Sydney, ca. 1875–1901] C H Woolcott, Town Clerk, albumen photoprint, State Library of New South Wales.

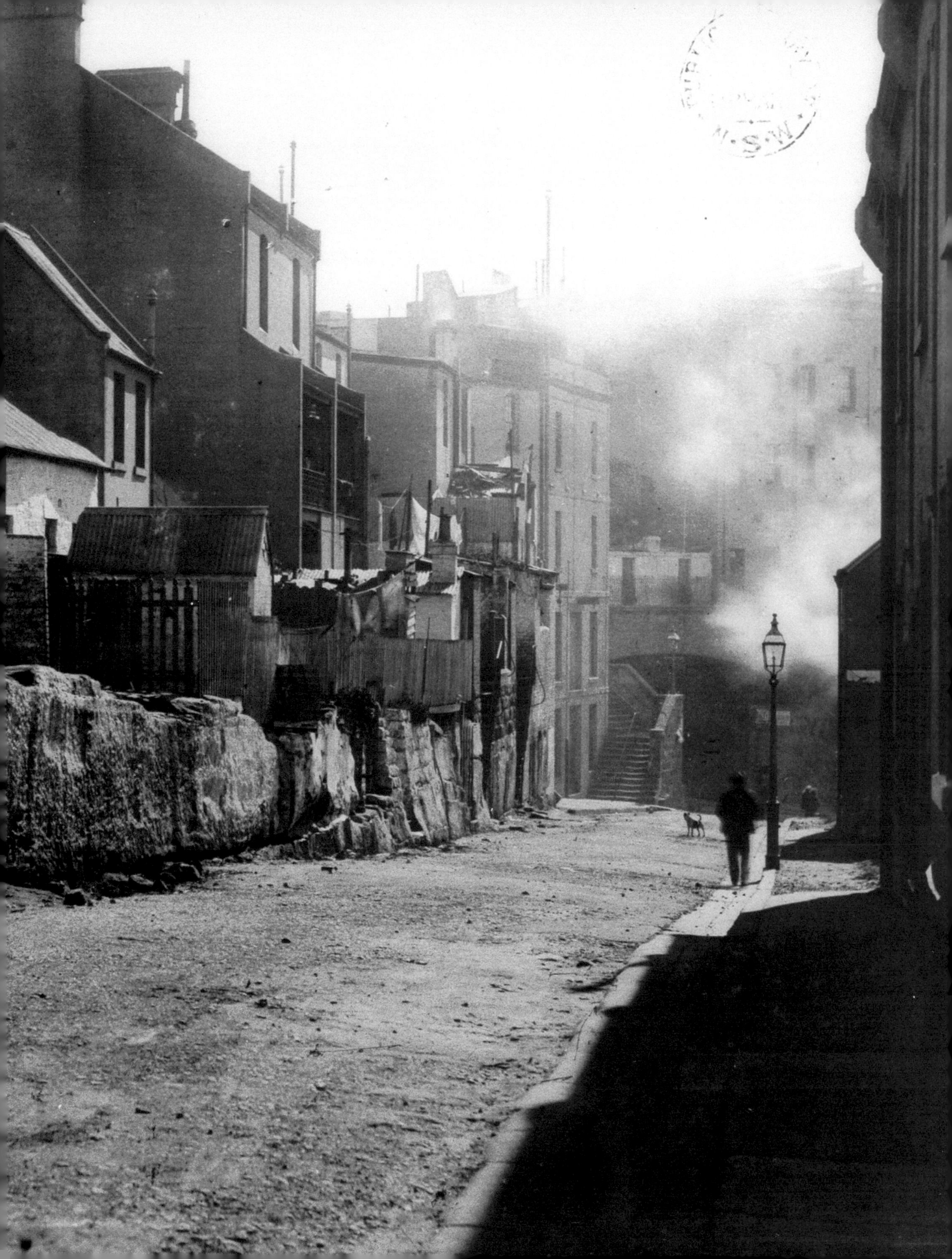
N·S·W

FROM THE GROUND UP

Rear of Susannah Place, Sydney Rocks Area: photographs, Cumberland Place, Sept 1901 No 21, New South Wales Department of Public Works, 1901, albumen photoprint, Mitchell Library, State Library of New South Wales

top left [Susannah Place] Housing Commission, 3/1948, dry plate, Government Printing Office collection, State Library of New South Wales **top right** Gloucester Street looking south, 1962, photographer unknown, Susannah Place Museum Collection, Historic Houses Trust **bottom left** Gloucester Street, photograph Robert Willson, September 1966, Mitchell Library, State Library of New South Wales **bottom right** [Susannah Place] Housing Commission, 3/1948, dry plate, Government Printing Office collection, State Library of New South Wales

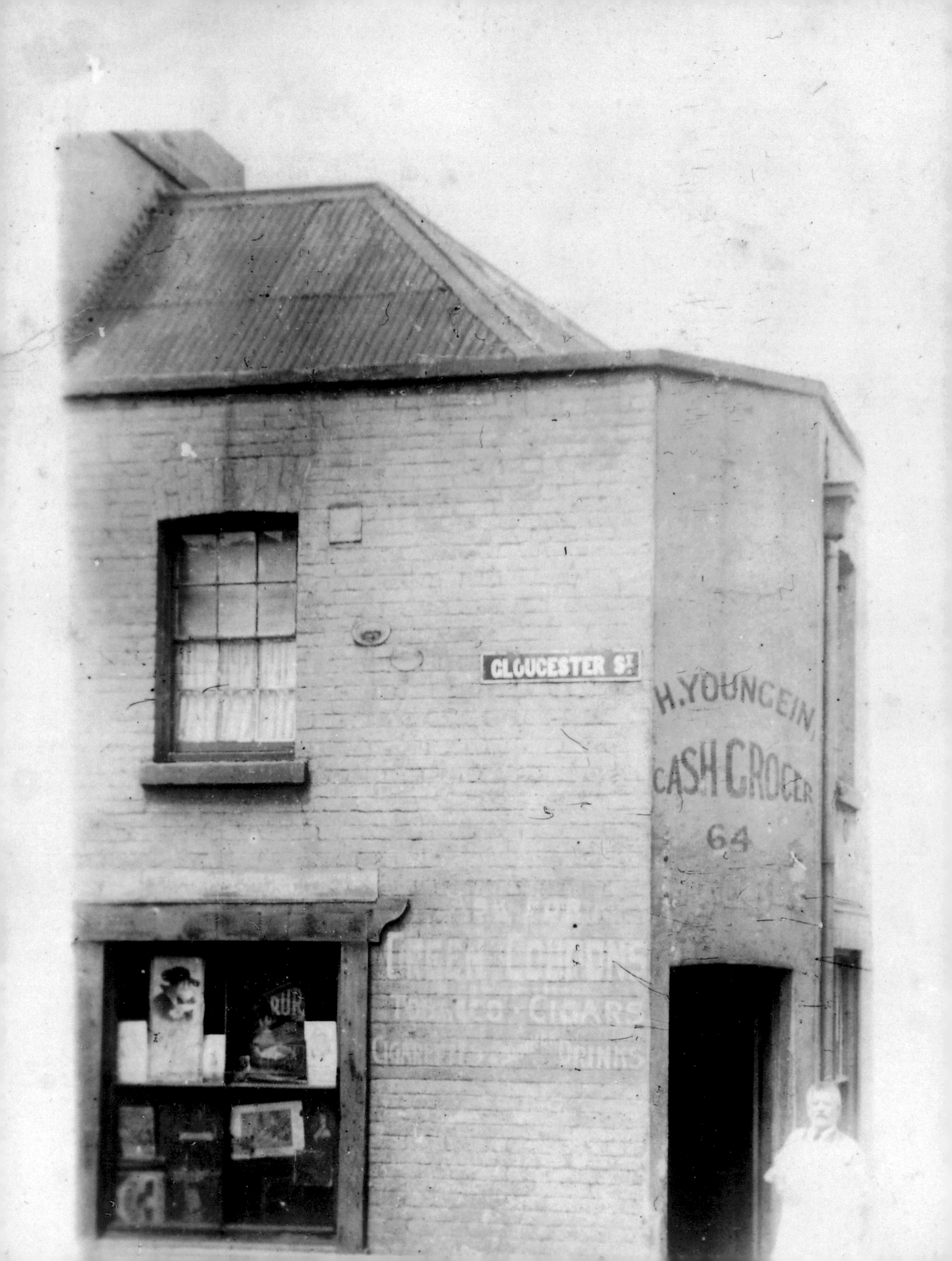
GLOUCESTER St.
H. YOUNGEIN,
CASH GROCER
64

Sugar was delivered to the shop on the horse wagon and they used to carry it down the side then put it in the cellar ... my father had bought a piano case – when pianos were imported into Australia they were imported in wooden cases that were tin lined and he bought one of these, and the sugar used to be placed in there to save it from the rats and vermin that was in those old homes at Susannah Place.

The shop had a window which was fairly large ... onto Gloucester Street ... my mother used to have lollies on show there for the children and there was a small blind that she used to pull down because of the afternoon sun to protect the lollies ... [24]

James Young (Youngein), 1990. Tenant No 64 Gloucester Street, 1904–17

Hugo Youngein (Lyunggren), c1920s. Courtesy R Younger **background** Excerpt from George Hill bankruptcy file, 1887, Supreme Court, Insolvency Files, State Records NSW **opposite** Hugo Youngein poses outside his 'Cash Grocer', No 64 Gloucester Street. c1920s. Courtesy Young family

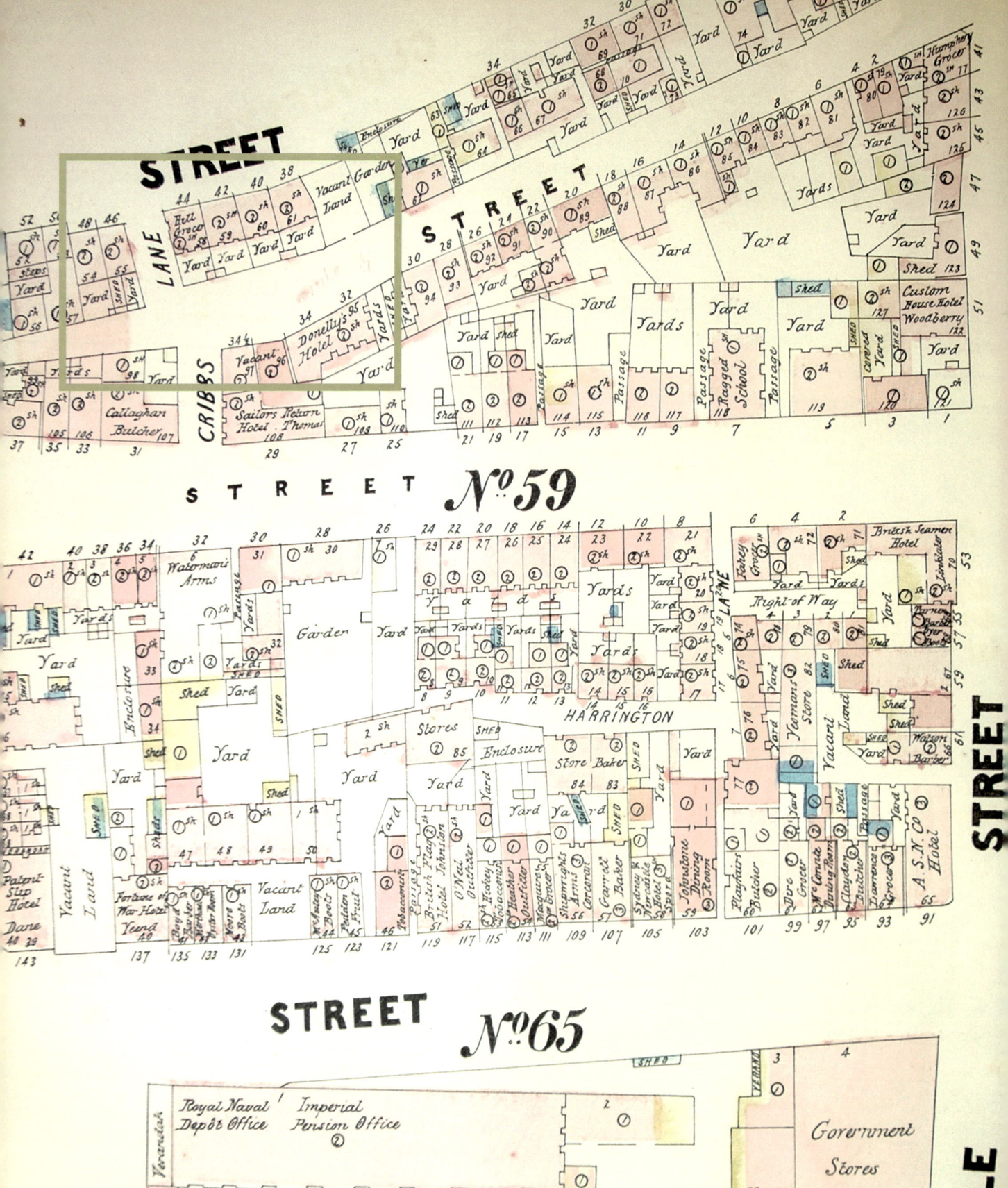

Map — No. 59 and No. 65 blocks, bounded by Argyle Street, Harrington Street, Cribbs Lane, and adjoining streets. Notable labels include: Humphrey Grocer, Custom House Hotel Woodberry, Ragged School, Hill Grocer, Donelly's Hotel, Callaghan Butcher, Sailors Return Hotel Thomas, Waterman's Arms, British Seamen Hotel, Fortune of War Hotel Yeend, British Flag Hotel Johnston, O'Neil Outfitter, Hickey Tobacconist, Maguire's Boot, Shipwrights Arms Cordeiral, Garratt Baker, Sydney Mercantile, Johnstone Dining Room, Playfair's, Doe Grocer, McConnells Boarding House, Clayden Butcher, Lawrence Grocer, A.S.N. Co Hotel, Yeaman's Store, Watson Barber, Patent Slip Hotel Dane, Royal Naval Depôt Office, Imperial Pension Office, Government Stores.

FROM THE GROUND UP

1. Peter Tonkin, 'City of Dionysus', in Peter Emmett, *Sydney: metropolis, suburb, harbour*, Historic Houses Trust, Sydney, 2000, p3.
2. *Sydney Gazette*, 15 May 1803.
3. Dr John Cobley (ed), *Sydney Cove 1788: the first year of the settlement of Australia*, Hodder & Stoughton, London, 1962, p248.
4. J T Bigge, *Report of the Commissioner of Inquiry, on the state of agriculture and trade in the Colony of New South Wales*, London, 1823, Australiana Facsimile Editions No 70, Libraries Board of South Australia, Adelaide, 1966, p42.
5. Peter Cunningham, *Two years in New South Wales: a series of letters, comprising sketches of the actual state of that colony, of its peculiar advantages to emigrants, of its topography, natural history*, David S Macmillan (ed), Angus & Robertson, Sydney, 1966, p28 (first published in 1827).
6. 'Stray leaves from the journal of a wanderer in Australia', diary of Felton Mathew, 1829. Transcribed and published on the Internet by Bruce Jones, <http://www.users.bigpond.com/narrabeen/feltonmatthews/stray.htm>. Manuscript held by National Library of Australia, Call No: MS 15.
7. J T Bigge, *Report of the Commissioner of Inquiry, on the state of agriculture and trade in the Colony of New South Wales*, p42.
8. Register entry No 228 d.1820: – Conway, Department of Lands NSW.
9. Memorials forwarded by the Commissioner of Claims 1832–42, State Records NSW, Reel 1207.
10. Town Grant 1A 47, p50, Land Titles Office.
11. *Sydney Morning Herald*, 4 July 1842.
12. Isadore Brodsky, *The streets of Sydney*, Old Sydney Free Press, Sydney, 1962, pp20–1.
13. Ruth Park, *The companion guide to Sydney*, Collins, Sydney, 1973, p67.
14. Reverend Henry Carmichael, *New South Wales Magazine*, 1834.
15. Entitlement certificates of Edward and Mary Riley and Susannah Sterne, State Records NSW, 4/4828.
16. 1845 Rate Assessment Book, City of Sydney Archives.
17. ibid
18. Stefan Muthesius, *The English terraced house*, Yale University Press, New Haven and London, 1982, p79.
19. Eliza Walker & S K Johnstone, 'Old Sydney in the 'forties: Recollections of Lower George Street and "The Rocks"', *Journal of Royal Australian Historical Society*, vol 16, 1930, p307.
20. William Stanley Jevons, 'Remarks upon the social map of Sydney, 1858', manuscript, Microfilm CY 1045, Mitchell Library, State Library of New South Wales, pp20–1.
21. Select Committee on the Condition of the Working Classes of the Metropolis, Minutes of evidence, *Votes and Proceedings of the Legislative Assembly of New South Wales*, 1859–60, vol 4, p78.
22. Select Committee on the Condition of the Working Classes of the Metropolis, Minutes of evidence, p169.
23. Will of Mary Riley, NSW Supreme Court Series 2/1095.
24. James Young (Youngein) oral history, 1990.

left Linoleum c1960, No 64 Gloucester Street veranda kitchen, 2005, photograph © Ross Heathcote **centre** No 64 Gloucester Street (shop) wall (detail), 2004, photograph © Ross Heathcote **right** Martin Andersen (right) standing outside No 64 Gloucester Street, late 1940s. Courtesy Terri Williams **opposite** H P Dove, *A new and complete wharf, street and building plan directory of the city of Sydney*, 1880, Museum of Sydney collection, Historic Houses Trust. [Nos 38–44 in box show location of Susannah Place]

59

We used to have running races and go around the block, around the hotel, around Little Essex Street and back…[1]

Patricia Thomas, 1993. Tenant No 62 Gloucester Street, 1933–42

AROUND

3

THE BLOCK

The Rocks of Patricia Thomas's childhood has changed dramatically since the late 1930s, much of it becoming obscured or lost over the years. The Australian Hotel is still on the corner but Little Essex Street was demolished in the 1950s to make way for the Cahill Expressway.

The identity of Susannah Place has been inextricably bound to this picturesque harbourside neighbourhood and the robust community that settled there. Many of the streets and laneways in The Rocks, formed during the early years of the colony, were constructed haphazardly, dictated by need and terrain rather than any thoughts of town planning. As historian Charles Bertie described in 1911:

> When roads became a necessity they were made to fit the scene ... roads jostled and elbowed each other, ran up precipices and disappeared or dropped down to merge in the main highway.[2]

The higher streets like Gloucester and Cumberland, which perched on the sandstone cliffs, enjoyed a 'splendid view of the harbour' and its 'free and fresh sea breezes'.[3] Writing of life in New South Wales in the 1830s, English author Alexander Harris found The Rocks, being 'elevated and almost surrounded by the waters of the harbour', was 'the pleasantest part of Sydney' and 'when George Street (the main business street) is like an oven, a fine soft breeze may generally be felt moving on that high ground'.[4]

In 1844 the 'much frequented and well-known public house' the St Patrick's Inn, located opposite Susannah Place, was advertised for sale. The auction notice 'to persons in search of a safe investment of capital' described the magnificent views the future owner could enjoy:

> In no part of Sydney is the view from this surpassed. It embraces as a panorama Government House, its grounds, and walks — Macquarie place — St James's, — Surry Hills — the whole eastern side of the City ... It also commands ... Pinchgut — South Head and headlands of the harbour; bearing back again the eye is arrested by Waverly, Mrs Darling's Point, the splendid mansions of Sir Thomas Mitchell, Pott's Point, Craigend, Darlinghurst, and all the other innumerable residences and splendid grounds belonging to the opulent and distinguished of our Sydney proprietary.[5]

The views of the harbour, despite changes to the skyline, were no less splendid for 20th-century tenants of Susannah Place like Ellen Marshall, who describes the

A by-way to George Street, 1906, Harold Cazneaux, glass negative. Reproduced courtesy Cazneaux family and National Library of Australia **previous page** *The Rocks and Harbour Bridge* (detail), Sali Herman, 1970, oil on canvas. Private collection, South Australia, © Estate of the artist. Photograph courtesy Deutscher-Menzies

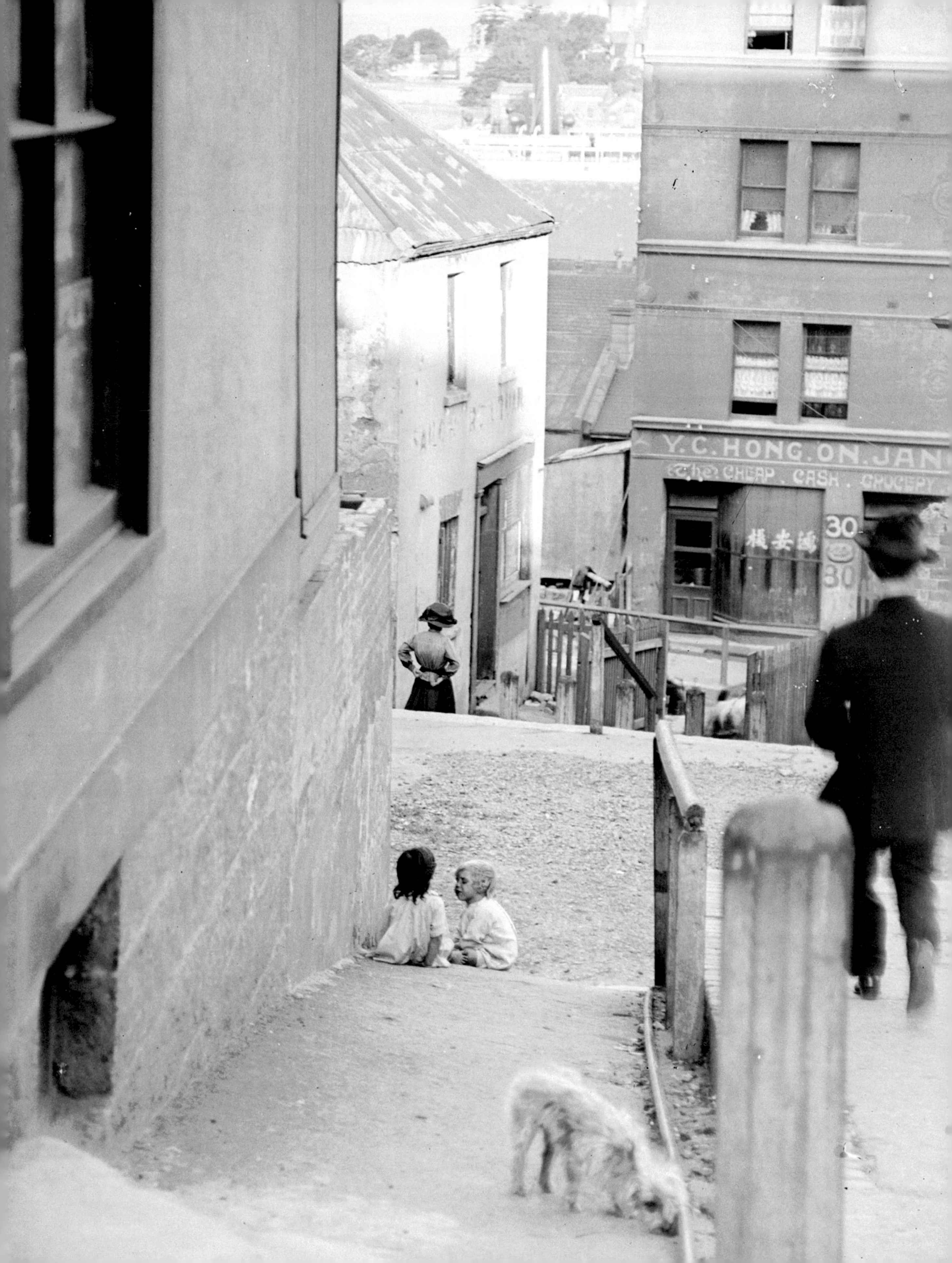
Y.C. HONG. ON. JAN
The CHEAP . CASH .
30
30

views from her back door and bedroom window when she lived in No 62 from 1962:

> We had the Harbour Bridge on our left looking north and it used to shine in the window. We could see the Governor's residence through the trees in the Botanic Gardens and Fort Denison. On a hot night you could sit here and watch the lights going blink blink, green and red. We even used to look into the zoo with binoculars and see the animal enclosures. We used to see the Customs House clock and of course we could see the Opera House being built. We were never without a breeze; even on the hottest night you'd get some air movement off the water.[6]

By the time Ellen left The Rocks in 1990 the construction of apartments in Harrington Street had completely obliterated the harbour views and absorbed the section of open ground in Cambridge Street known to locals as the 'drying green' (a reference to the period from the early 1900s until the 1970s when clothes lines were a regular feature on the site). Cambridge Street itself had long ago stopped being a thoroughfare. In pictures from the early 1900s it is shown populated with children and goats. At the southern end, the yards of Susannah Place extended out into the street and the remaining narrow strip of road became a playground for local children, their cries of 'are you going down the back lane?' echoing for many years.[7]

As William Stanley Jevons observed in the 1850s, the streets and laneways of The Rocks were extensions of people's houses and their lives spilled out into them: 'In the higher parts of the Rocks, Gloucester and Cumberland Streets, there was a very little more stir, a few people gossiping at the corners, or moving homewards'.[8] They were places to talk to neighbours and exchange news and gossip, to hang washing and for children to play in. Very little changed in the first half of the 20th century. The area's regular inhabitants included numerous street sellers with their horsedrawn carts, the clothes prop man, Chinese hawkers selling household linens, the rabbito who would skin the rabbits while customers waited, the milkman and the iceman.

Ron Thompson, born in The Rocks in 1933, fondly remembered the clever cries of Jacko the fruit and vegetable seller who would call, 'peas young and green' and 'lettuces with hearts like heroes'.[9] Ron's older sister, Patricia, looked forward to the

Cambridge Street, The Rocks, 1902, Sophie Steffanoni, oil on canvas, Caroline Simpson Library & Research Collection, Historic Houses Trust

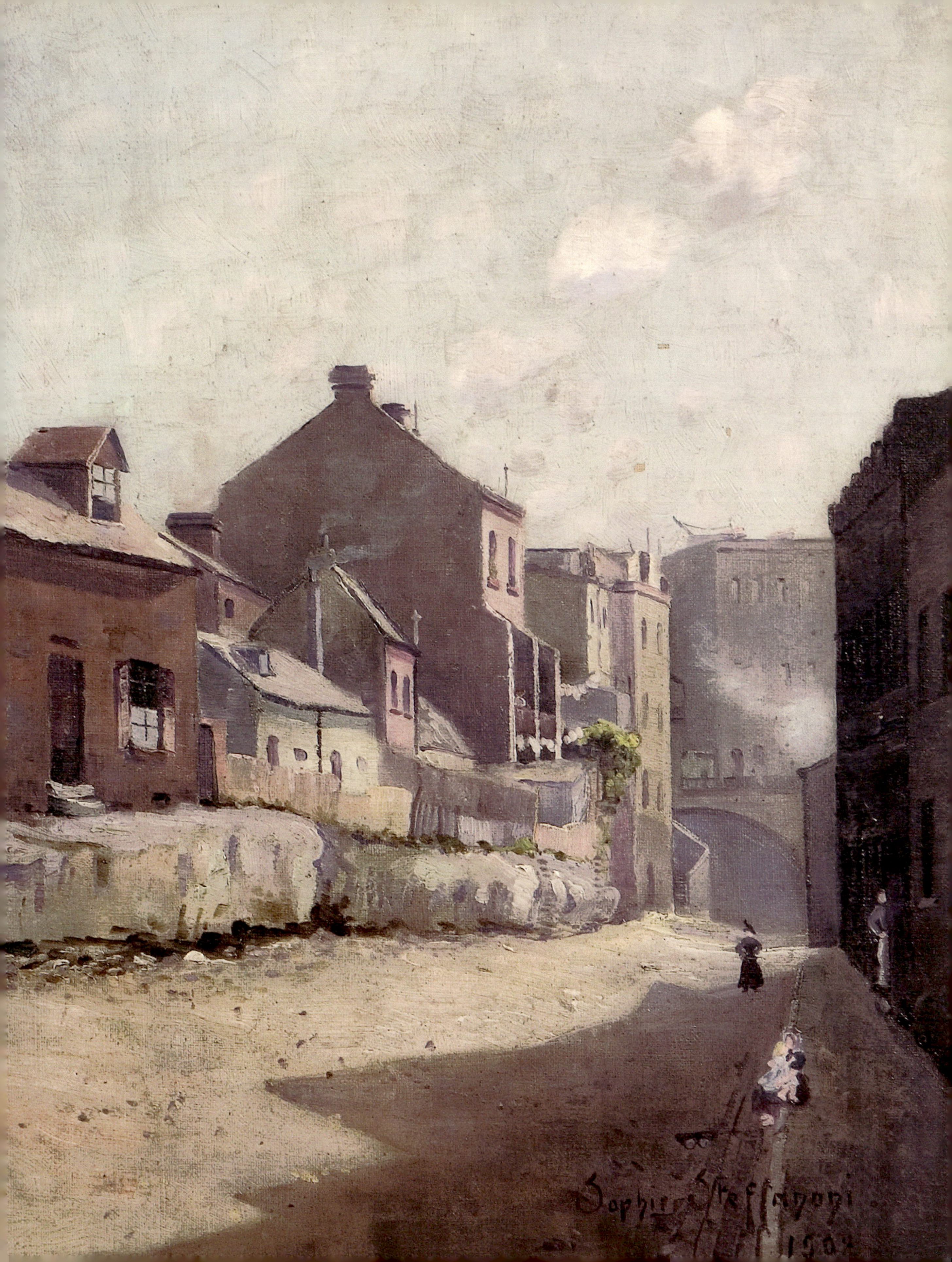

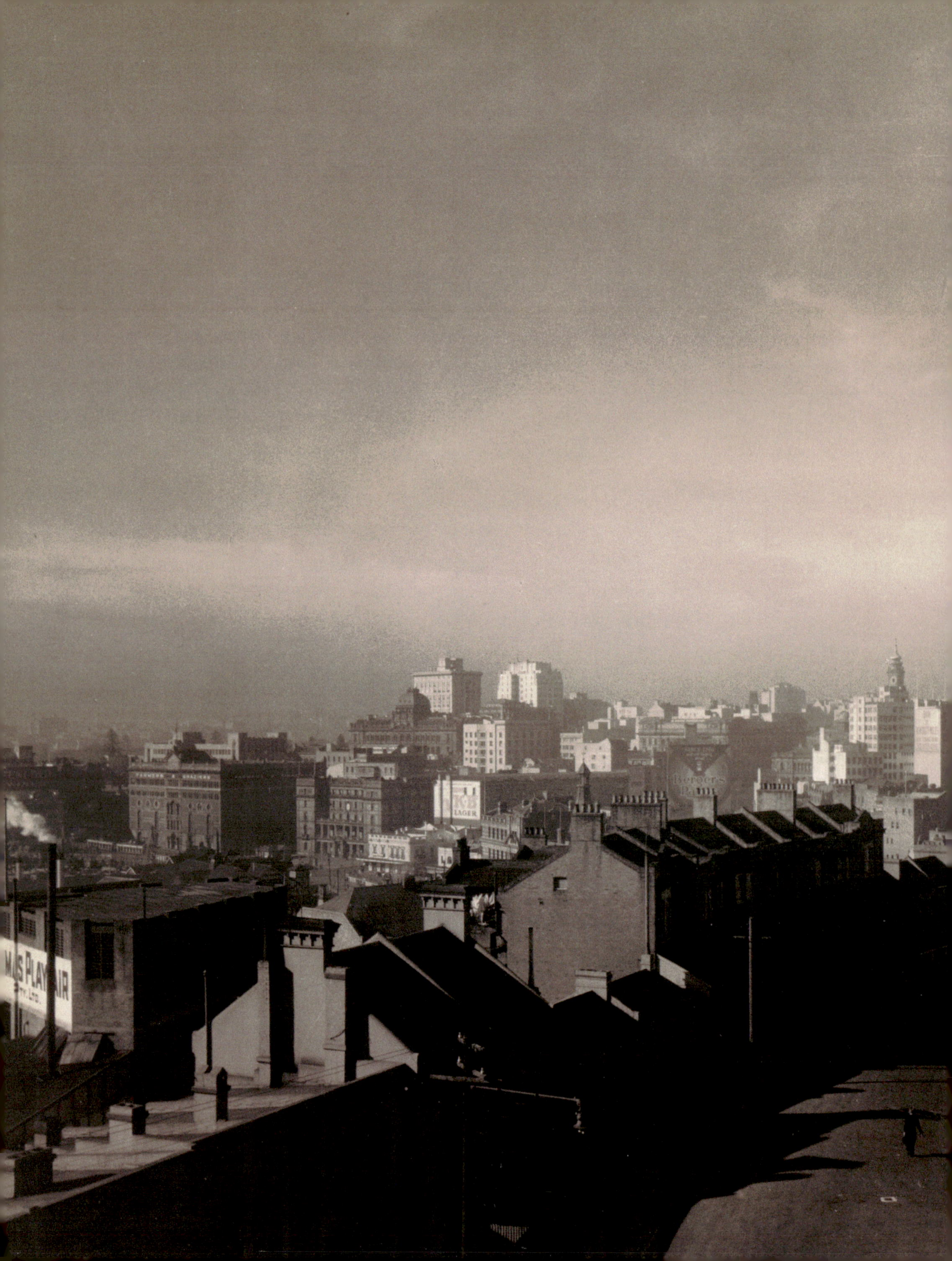
LAGER

AROUND THE BLOCK

Sydney from the Rocks, photograph Max Dupain, 1938, gelatin silver photograph. Gift of Edron Pty Ltd, 1995, through the auspices of Alistair McAlpine, Art Gallery of New South Wales

67

There was a lot of demolition work going on opposite our place [when I was young] — a huge area in which the places had been condemned and pulled down because of the vermin and the rats.[10]

James Young, 1990. Tenant No 64 Gloucester Street, 1904–17

daily visit by the baker: 'If any of us were home sick we'd always stand at the front door because we knew the baker would give us a lovely fresh crusty roll'. There were also the sounds that drifted up from the waterfront: 'the tremendous roar'[11] of the coal dropping into the hull of a ship; the anchors being winched up; and the sounds of the different ships' horns.

James Young (Youngein) was only six months old when his family's house was demolished in the large-scale 'slum' clearances that followed the 1900 outbreak of bubonic plague. Forced to relocate, the Youngeins moved across the road into the vacant corner shop and house at Susannah Place, from where they witnessed the protracted demolition of over 30 buildings between Gloucester and Cumberland streets. The government acted quickly to stop the spread of the plague. Affected areas of the city were barricaded and quarantined, and anyone suspected of carrying the disease, and their 'contacts', were taken to the Quarantine Station at North Head. A bounty of sixpence was paid for each rat caught. Local men who were restricted from leaving the quarantined areas were employed to carry out the cleansing operations on buildings that were not demolished, like Susannah Place. In 1901 the state government resumed the entire Rocks area, effectively becoming its sole landlord.

The Youngein family were one in a line of shopkeepers who ran the 'cheap cash grocer' from the front room of No 64. Operating from 1844 to 1935, the shop supplied household groceries to the local neighbourhood and during difficult times the Youngeins would offer their customers 'tick', or credit. Their son recalled the intermittent work of wharf workers meant that 'they'd have to wait a week for one day's wages'.[12]

Iceman, Frederick Danvers Power: photonegatives, 1898–1926, glass photonegative, State Library of New South Wales

69

Feather dusters used to be delivered by the Chinese hawkers. They used to come round regularly with all sorts of goods – brooms and feather dusters – they used to carry them banded together, tied together at the end of a piece of rope that they carried over their shoulders. And they carried baskets, which included linens and sheeting. They used to call in at the shop because I remember quite well they were such humble people ... my father and mother would talk to them for quite a while as they knew more about the business in that area than anyone ... they knew which were good streets for business and bad streets.[13]

James Young, 1990. Tenant No 64 Gloucester Street, 1904–17

[Chinese carrying shoulder baskets, The Rocks, Sydney] 1886, Livingston Hopkins, etching, National Library of Australia

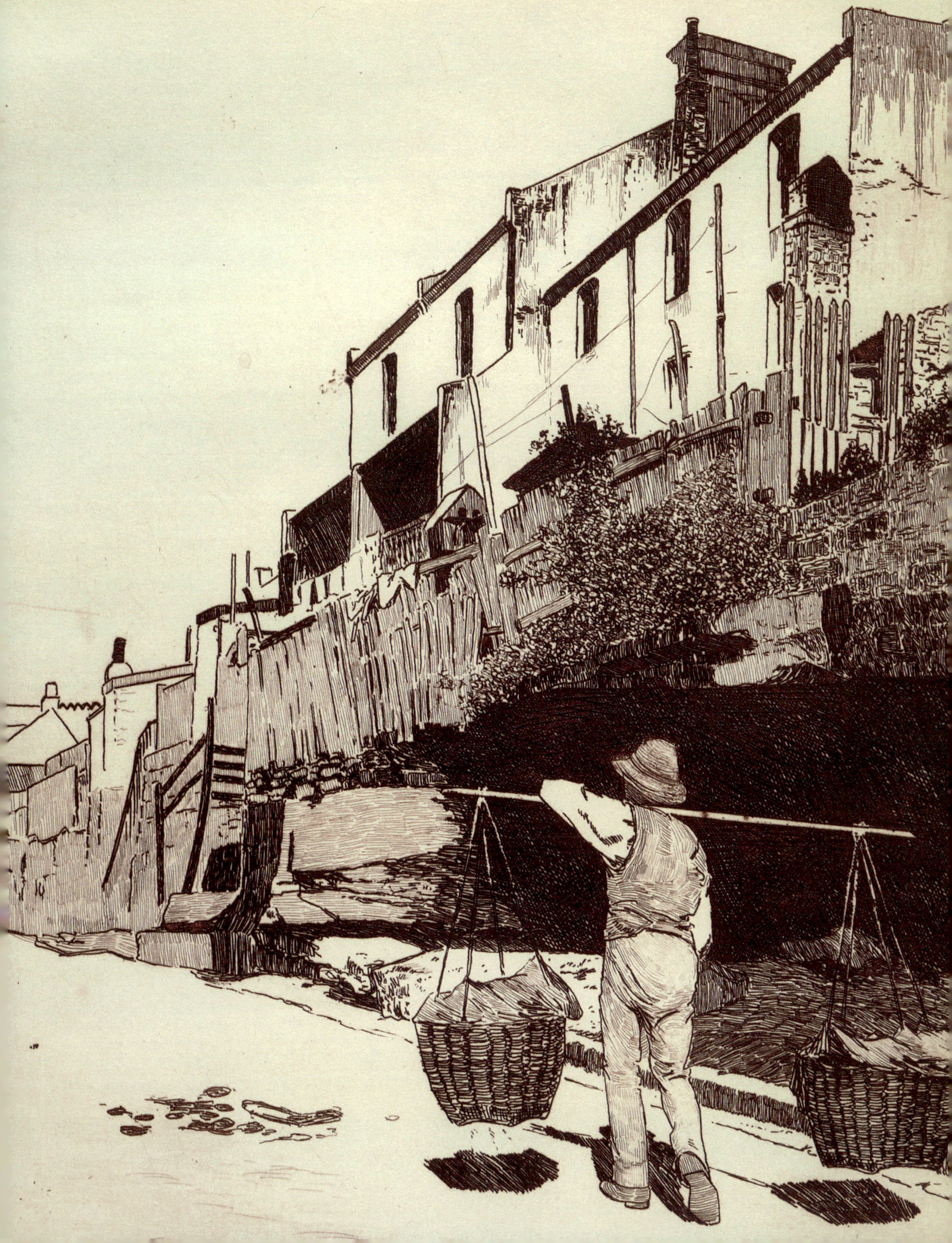

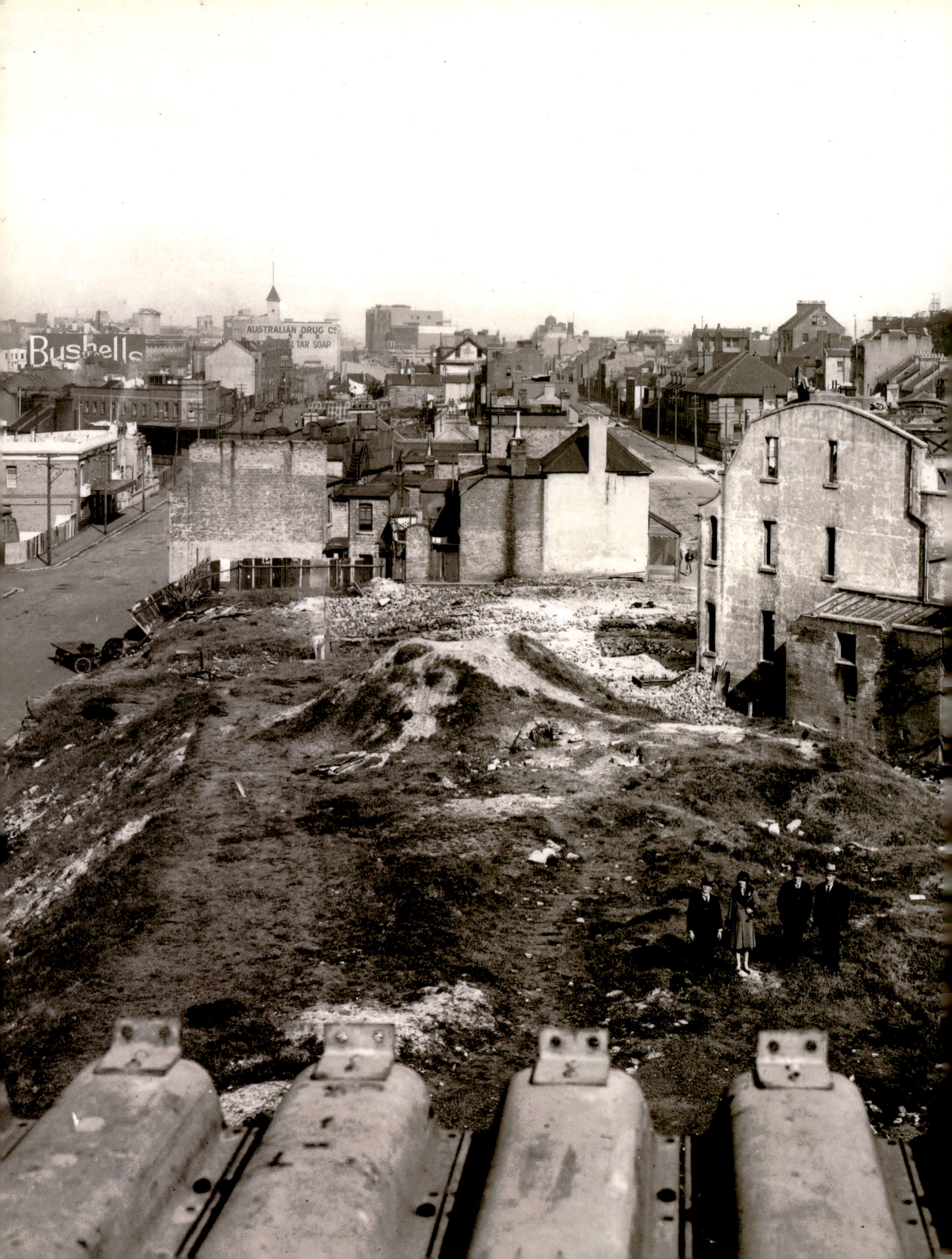
Bushells
AUSTRALIAN DRUG Co
TAR SOAP

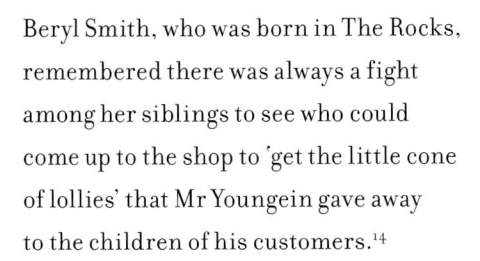

Beryl Smith, who was born in The Rocks, remembered there was always a fight among her siblings to see who could come up to the shop to 'get the little cone of lollies' that Mr Youngein gave away to the children of his customers.[14]

Years later in the late 1950s Beryl lived in No 64 with her own children. The shop, long gone, was replaced with her lounge room. At Christmas time Beryl would have a Christmas tree in the room under which were presents for her family and a small bag of lollies for the each of the children in the street. She remembers their eagerness on Christmas morning:

> The kids would come at five in the morning, 'Oh Mrs Smith, when can we get our present?' I'd put my head out the top window, 'would you go away and come back later?' But they'd be back in ten minutes.[15]

The people of The Rocks had barely breathed a sigh of relief after the plague clearances before the neighbourhood was once again faced with more demolitions, this time to make way for the long anticipated bridge that would connect the two sides of the harbour. Hundreds of buildings in The Rocks and Millers Point that stood in the path of the Sydney Harbour Bridge and its approaches were demolished, and countless residents displaced in this already overcrowded neighbourhood. The dramatic 1927 photograph (opposite) documents the progress of the bridge as it slowly swallowed up houses along Princes Street, a street that no longer exists. For the residents in nearby streets the day-to-day mess and noise from the demolitions and subsequent years of construction must have been relentless. On days when it all became too much, grocer Hugo Youngein would close the shop at No 64.

The construction chaos during the 1930s was viewed by the neighbourhood children from quite a different perspective. For young Patricia Thomas the houses that had been pulled down behind Susannah Place were a source of entertainment:

> There was a nightwatchman who used to sit there every night with a fire and we kids used to go down there and talk to him and take potatoes down if we had any and he'd put them in the fire. We'd sit around eating them.[16]

In 1935 the Sydney City Council built the King George V playground for the children of the area on a strip of land running alongside the approach to the bridge.

Houses along Princes Street in the path of the Harbour Bridge construction. View looking south from end of span No 1 showing property to be demolished, 28 June 1927, State Records NSW

The pub and the home were the centres of the social scene and the hatching grounds of the networks of neighbourly support that helped to sustain and unite the community.[17]

Shirley Fitzgerald and Christopher Keating, 1991

Childhood friends Ron Thompson and David Hamilton recalled that the boys and girls were separated and the boys' supervisor, 'Skipper', would open up on weekends and during school holidays when there were 'building blocks, a bit of a library, racquet ball, cricket and … free milk'.[18] Years later, Ron proudly presented Susannah Place Museum with his Certificate of Athletic Proficiency, awarded in 1948. Most children attended the local schools – Fort Street Public School, St Brigid's and St Patrick's. Their proximity meant the children could come home for lunch. Patricia Thomas who attended St Patrick's would often come home to No 62 to make herself bread and jam sandwiches.

Unlike the Harbour Bridge, which has become a much-loved Sydney icon, the Cahill Expressway has been variously described as a 'bland concrete motorway', 'a monolithic affront to urban sensitivity'[19] and 'a monument to civic planning of the most offensive kind'.[20] The expressway, which opened in 1962, cut Gloucester Street in two, obliterating still more Rocks housing in its wake. Yet, for Beryl Smith and her family of five the demolition of her one-bedroom house in Cambridge Street was a blessing as she was put on a list and relocated to Susannah Place. Ron Thompson and David Hamilton made the most of the construction work, playing in the huge stormwater drains being laid, and Ron Smith 'lifted' some of the bricks from the building site to create a little garden bed in the backyard of No 64. Despite the continual reshaping of the neighbourhood by external forces, the community just got on with their lives.

No matter what time we step back into, we would find the ever-present public house or 'pub'. In the immediate vicinity of Susannah Place was St Patrick's Inn (later renamed the Whalers Arms). Just across the road, a few houses along to the south were the Ship and Mermaid and the Bird in Hand (formerly the Turk's Head) and further still, where the Cahill Expressway is today, were the Black Dog and the Ocean Wave. To the north on the corner of Cumberland Street was the Australian Hotel and behind it in Cambridge Street stood the Cambridge Hotel. Of course, not all of these pubs were operating at the same time; they came and went over the years, their names changing along with their publicans. In the 1930s, 'there were fights on just about every corner when the hotels closed at 6 o'clock but we were all taught to ignore that sort of thing'.[21]

Sydney Rocks Area: photographs, Cambridge Street No 9, Department of Public Works, 1901, albumen photoprint, Mitchell Library, State Library of New South Wales

THE ROCKS
THIS OR THAT

AROUND THE BLOCK

Today we cannot imagine The Rocks without its historic buildings and back lanes, yet it wasn't very long ago that governments and town planners wanted to create a modern entrance to the city of Sydney:

> *The opportunity to rebuild part of Sydney occurs, not because war has destroyed it, but because peace-time pressures brought about by surging development have necessitated a new conception to meet the expansion of the great metropolis of Sydney.*[22]

In 1970 the Sydney Cove Redevelopment Authority (SCRA) was given control of The Rocks with a charter to restore, renovate and redevelop the area with high-rise offices, shops and hotels. Faced with higher rents, poor property maintenance and pressure from the authority to move, the community formed the Rocks Residents Action Group and enlisted the support of the NSW Builders Labourers Federation (BLF) to oppose the authority's development plans. By 1973 the BLF, under the leadership of Jack Mundey, had imposed green bans and halted demolition and construction in the area. However, by this time as more and more tenants left the area, the strong community that once existed slowly started to weaken. By 1974 Ellen and Dennis Marshall were the only tenants left at Susannah Place and the houses to the south along Gloucester Street to the Cahill Expressway were all empty. From Ellen's memory, 'It was like living on a five-acre property because we had nobody until the Cahill Expressway'.[23]

The green bans were a qualified success; while they had saved 'the hard husk' of the area – the historic buildings – the working-class community was destroyed.[24] Nita McCrae, the spokesperson for the Rocks Residents Action Group, fiercely argued that The Rocks was more than just old buildings; it was also the people – the generations of families who had called it home.

View from Susannah Place of demolition and excavations, c1980s. Courtesy Ellen Marshall. **opposite** Members of the Rocks People's Plan Committee – residents and architects – proposed an alternative 'People's Plan' to the redevelopment of The Rocks. *This or That, People's Plan*, December 1972, Sydney Harbour Foreshore Authority

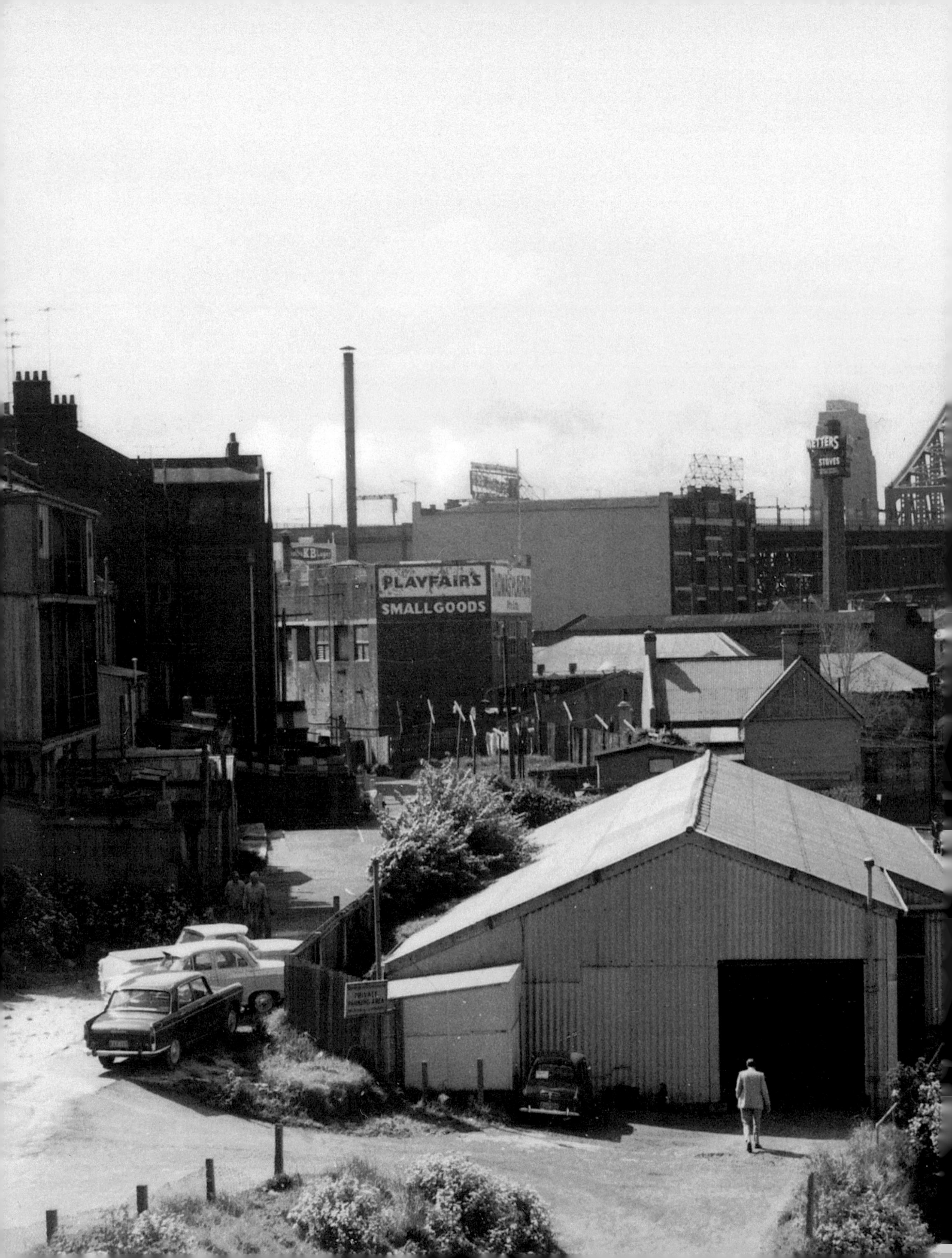
PLAYFAIR'S
SMALLGOODS
METTERS
STOVES

AROUND THE BLOCK

View over Harrington and
Cambridge Streets, Robert Willson,
September 1966, Mitchell Library,
State Library of New South Wales

79

AROUND THE BLOCK

left Sydney Rocks Area: photographs, Cambridge Street looking south from Cumberland Place No 17, Department of Public Works, 1901, albumen photoprints, Mitchell Library, State Library of New South Wales **top right** Sydney Rocks Area: photographs, Cambridge Street No 8, Department of Public Works, 1901, albumen photoprints, Mitchell Library, State Library of New South Wales **bottom right** Cambridge Street, Sydney, John Henry Harvey, 1907, toned glass lantern slide, State Library of Victoria

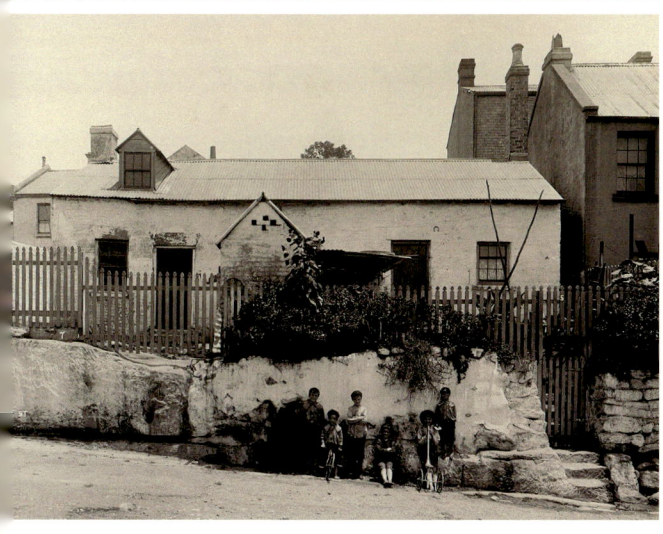

top left Gloucester Street looking north No 64 **top right** Cambridge Street looking to Argyle Cut No 13 August **bottom left** Cambridge Street. All three images from Sydney Rocks Area: photographs, Department of Public Works, 1901, albumen photoprints, Mitchell Library, State Library of New South Wales **bottom right** Gloucester Street and Cumberland Place, Sir Elliot Johnson, c1900, from a copy held in the Small Picture File collection, Mitchell Library, State Library of New South Wales

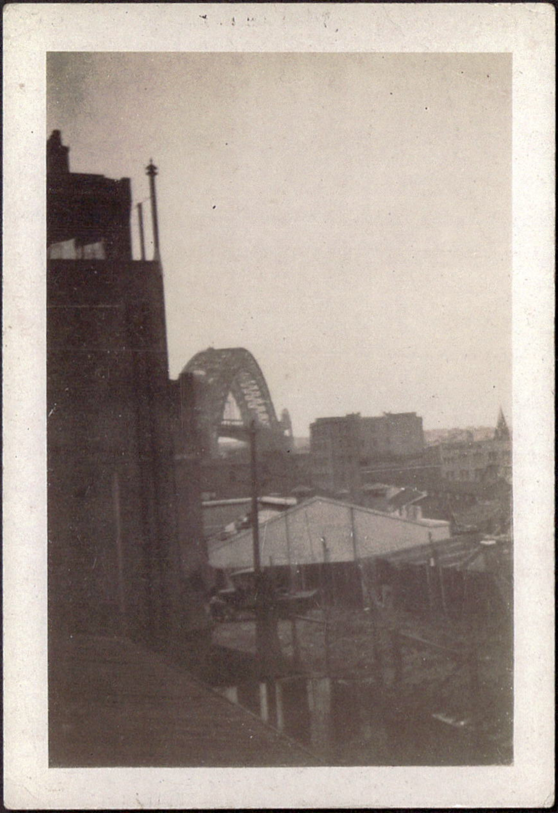

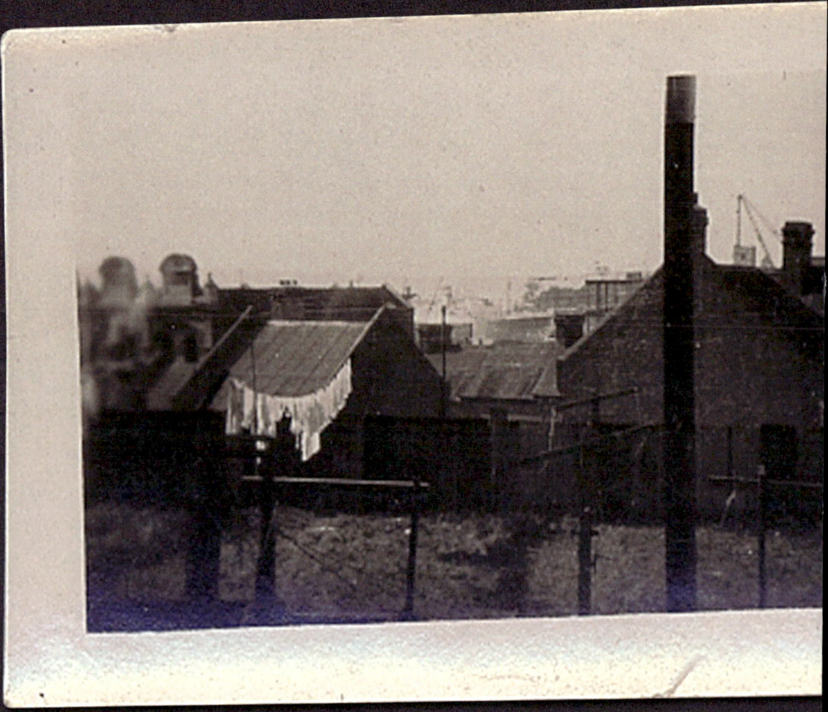

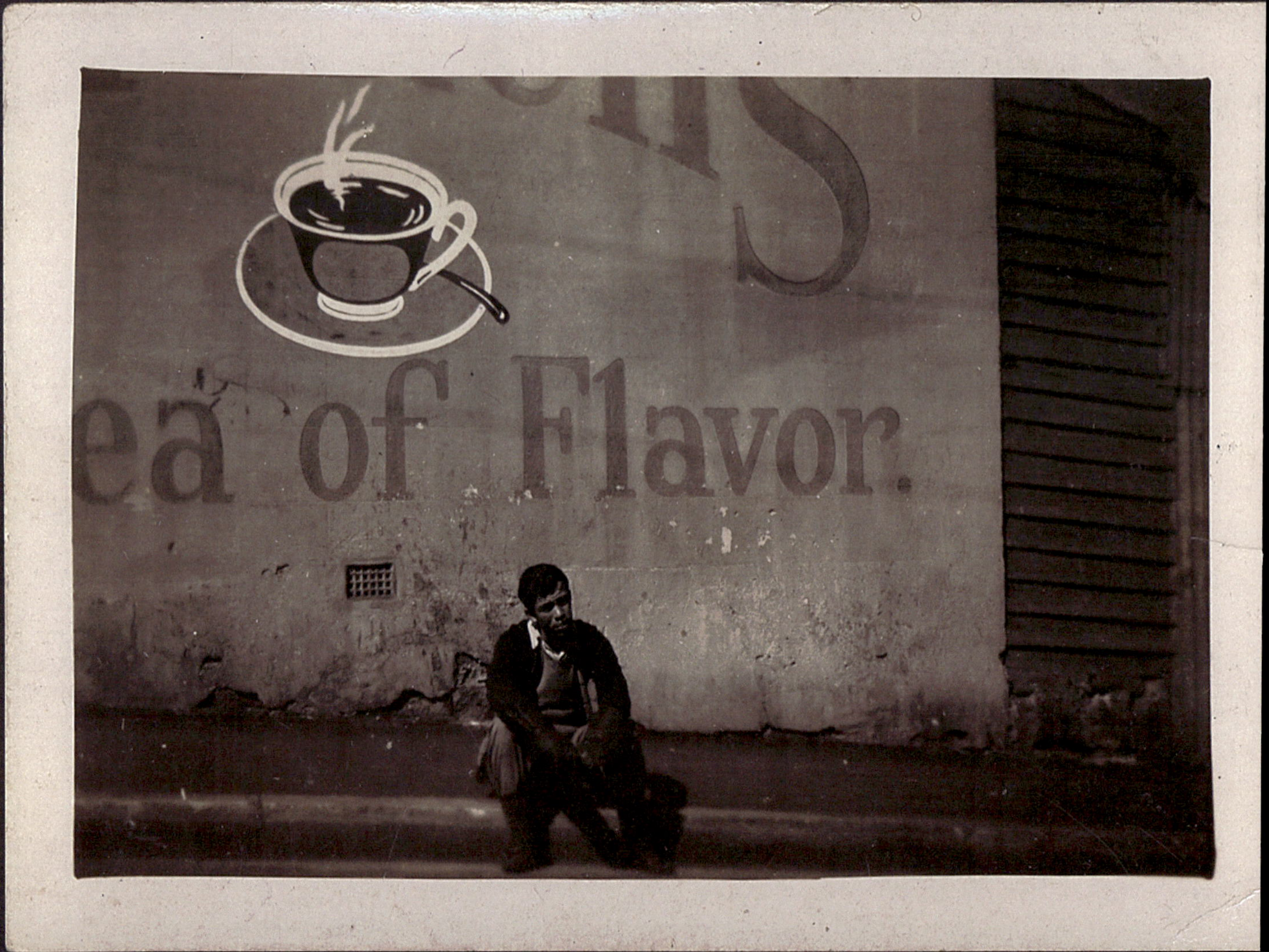
ea of Flavor.

My brother and myself used to sleep in the front bedroom ... I was always cranky about not being able to look out over the harbour.[25]

Ernie Andersen, 1990. Tenant No 64 Gloucester Street, 1937–49 and No 58, 1949–74

Jack Andersen and his younger brother Ernie were keen amateur photographers and used to process and develop their own negatives. Jack owned a Box Brownie camera and would take photographs of his parents, Girlie and Martin, and the views from Susannah Place. Jack took the photo of his mother and father (above) not long after his father had retired. It 'must have been a weekday,' recalls Jack, as 'dad is wearing his casual clothes and not his Sunday best'.

Girlie and Martin Andersen **opposite top** Views from Susannah Place **bottom** Bushells Tea Factory in Harrington Street. All photographs Jack Andersen, c1950s. Courtesy Jack Andersen

Sydney

AROUND THE BLOCK

1. Patricia Thomas (nee O'Brien/Thompson) oral history, 1993.
2. Charles Bertie, *Old Sydney*, Angus & Robertson Ltd, Sydney, 1911, p37.
3. *Sydney Morning Herald*, 17 February 1844.
4. Alexander Harris, *Settlers and convicts; or recollections of sixteen years' labour in the Australian backwoods*, Melbourne University Press, Melbourne, 1953, p49 (first published in London, 1847).
5. *Sydney Morning Herald*, 17 February 1844.
6. Ellen Marshall and Jenni Whitford oral history, 1992.
7. Patricia Thomas oral history, 1993.
8. William Stanley Jevons, 'Remarks upon the social map of Sydney, 1858', manuscript, Microfilm CY 1045, Mitchell Library, State Library of New South Wales, p33.
9. Ron Thompson and David Hamilton oral history, 2001.
10. James Young (Youngein) oral history, 1990.
11. Patricia Thomas oral history, 1993.
12. James Young (Youngein) oral history, 1990.
13. ibid
14. Beryl Smith (nee Kidd) oral history, 1993.
15. ibid
16. Patricia Thomas oral history, 1993.
17. Shirley Fitzgerald and Christopher Keating, *Millers Point: the urban village*, Hale & Iremonger, Sydney, 1991, p58.
18. Ron Thompson and David Hamilton oral history, 2001.
19. Sydney Architecture Walks, <http://www.sydneyarchitecture.org> and Rachel Crystal, 'Global City' in 'The Rocks' *Parallax*, One, Arcadia Press, Sydney, p30.
20. Max Kelly, *Anchored in a small cove: a history and archaeology of The Rocks, Sydney*, Sydney Cove Authority, Sydney, 1997, p103.
21. Patricia Thomas oral history, 1993.
22. Robert J Heffron, Premier of New South Wales, introduction in 'Most extensive redevelopment scheme', Sydney Harbour Foreshore Authority, c1964.
23. Ellen Marshall and Jenni Whitford oral history, 1993.
24. Grace Karskens, 'Tourists and pilgrims: (Re)visiting The Rocks, *Grit: Journal of Australian Studies*, Richard Nile (ed), no 78, 2003, p29.
25. Ernie Andersen oral history, 1990.

left Linoleum c1950, No 60 Gloucester Street kitchen, 2005, photograph © Ross Heathcote **centre** Jack Brown and Olive Jessie Young, c1940s. Residents of The Rocks. Courtesy Christine Hatchman **right** Southern wall (detail), No 64 Gloucester Street (shop), 2004, photograph © Ross Heathcote **opposite** Section of a panorama of The Rocks and Sydney Harbour, hand-coloured photograph Melvin Vaniman, 1907, Sydney Harbour Foreshore Authority

This is a private world. Behind the decent or defiant street face, behind the lamplit curtain, a personality as varied and as subtle as the human character itself is hidden.[1]

Lionel Brett, 1947

MAKING

4

a MARK

The evocative character of Susannah Place comes from its intact character as lived, used, loved and hated.[2]

Peter Emmett, 1989

Houses are such intimate spaces. Within them we nurture our children and dreams, close the door on our public life and enter our own private world, leaving traces of our lives and obscuring those of previous occupants – a layer of paint here, a nail in the wall there, a repair, a handrail worn smooth.

Between 1844 and 1990, over a hundred families have lived in the four houses of Susannah Place. Remarkably, while the surviving layers of paint, wallpapers and floor coverings and the evidence of modifications and repairs reflect the lifestyles of former occupants, the houses themselves have changed very little. Each of the houses is slightly different, with its own personality and story to tell. Stepping into the private world of Susannah Place one discovers how these houses were 'lived, used, loved and hated' over the years.

Like many other houses in the neighbourhood the Gloucester Street entrance to Susannah Place is not fronted by a garden.

Beyond the front door, with little ceremony (there is no hallway), we find ourselves in the parlour. William Stanley Jevons's descriptions of the domestic scenes he glimpsed through windows provide a rare insight into the 19th-century parlour:

> *The interior of all the dwellings, too, with few exceptions appeared cheerful where a glimpse could be obtained. The family was generally round the central table or sitting about on chairs & sofa. The females were generally engaged in needlework, all were talking.*[3]

Throughout the 19th century the parlour was set aside as the best room in the house. As architectural historian Stefan Muthesius observes in his book *The English terraced house*, 'the back room was for ordinary living and the front room for "best"'.[4] This 19th-century tradition was maintained by many of Susannah Place's 20th-century tenants. George Adaley's description of his grandmother's parlour in No 60 harks back to Jevons's description some 80 years earlier: 'The curtains

Layers of paint and wallpapers, No 58 Gloucester Street back room, 1991, photograph © Christopher Shain **previous page** Linoleum c1968, No 58 Gloucester Street basement kitchen (detail), 2004, photograph © Ross Heathcote

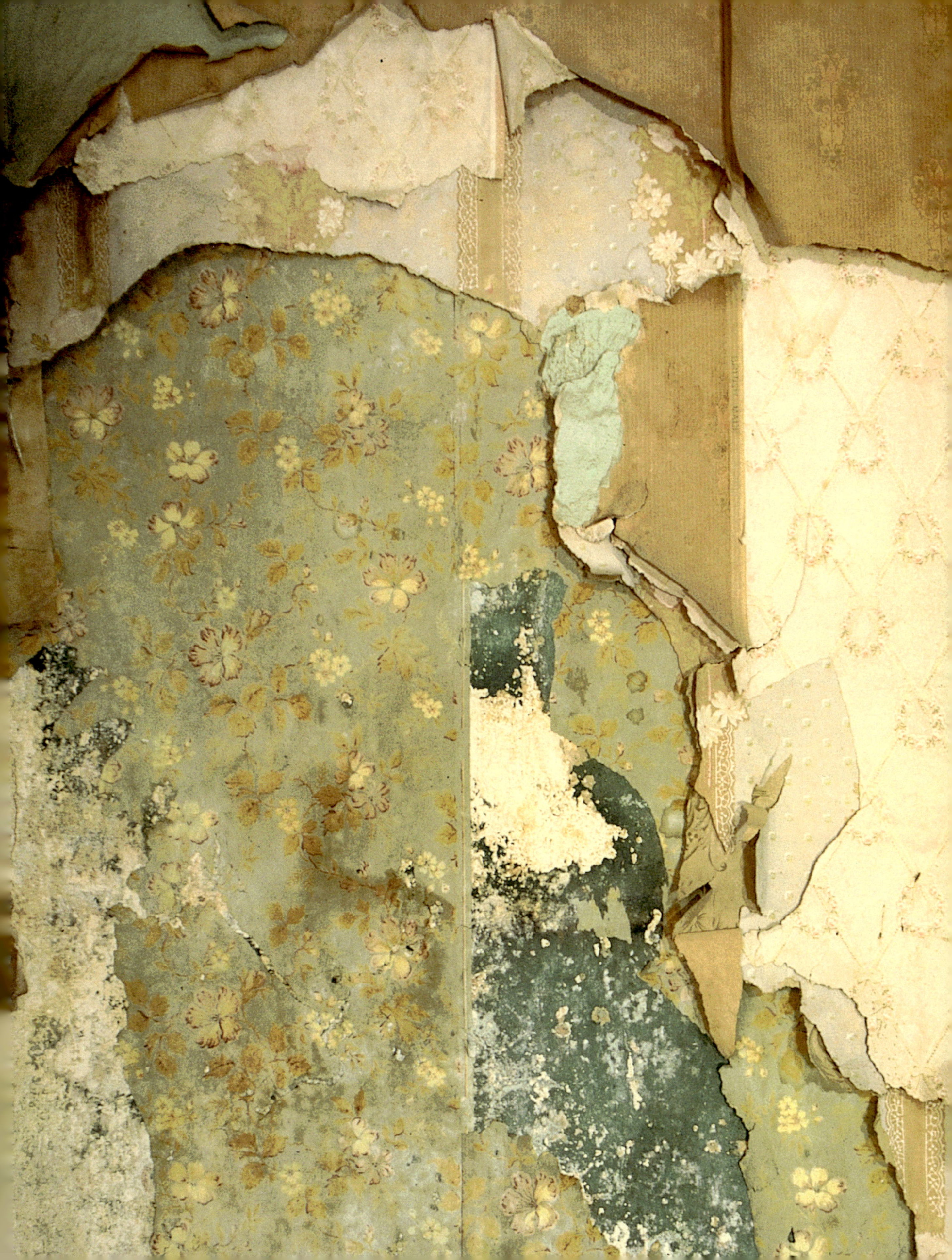

58

were drawn, it was always dark, a table with four chairs around it, a settee and a picture of my Uncle Emmanuel over the mantelpiece'.⁵

Despite the limited space in these small houses, the parlour was usually reserved for visitors and rarely used for everyday living. Growing up in No 64 in the 1930s, Jack Andersen recalls that the parlour 'was seldom used unless guests came in' and always had the 'blinds drawn halfway down'.⁶ Blinds generally served the dual purpose of providing privacy and protecting the furniture from sunlight.

At No 58, newly weds Florence and Leslie Gallagher, who lived with Leslie's grandmother, regarded the permanently darkened parlour as her special domain for displaying her most treasured possessions. Forbidden from using the front door, Les recalls they were 'supposed to go round the back … that front door was only for special people'.⁷ Jenni Whitford who lived in No 62 remembers it was the same in the 1960s:

> We always went round the back and sometimes if you knocked on the front door you'd hear this 'round the back' … the front door was for visitors, the families were meant to use the back.⁸

It must have been comforting for women like Margaret Thompson, who lived at No 62, to have a few special things, perhaps ornaments inherited from their mothers, to display in the parlour where they were safe from the daily wear and tear of family life. Margaret's daughter remembered the 'tables and chairs polished all the time' in readiness for visitors.⁹

Although each room in a house would have been designed for a prescribed use, in reality rooms were adapted to the circumstances of individual families. Jevons observed that the parlour often doubled as a bedroom at night by way of a

Leslie and Florence Gallagher with their daughter, Gloria, circa late 1940s. Tenants No 58 Gloucester Street, 1944–45. Courtesy Florence Gallagher **opposite** Front door, No 58 Gloucester Street, 2004, photograph © Ross Heathcote

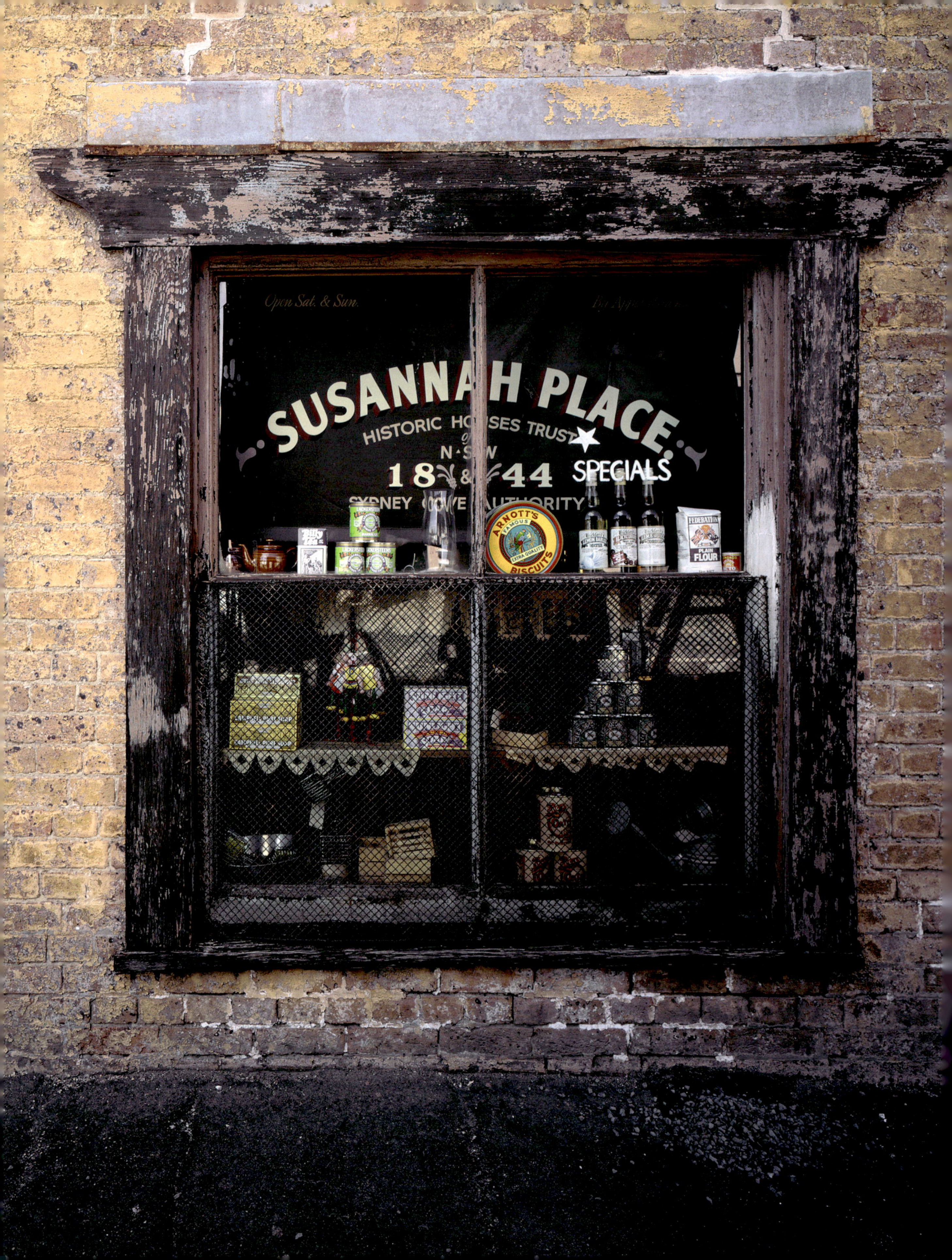

'gridiron' (a folding bed).[10] No doubt, by morning the room was righted again with everything returned to its proper place.

The families in Susannah Place lived frugally, using their few pieces of furniture until they fell apart and discarding them when they did. James Young recalled the lack of furniture and 'humbleness of the homes' of families he delivered groceries to in the early 1900s.[11] It was not uncommon for large pieces of furniture like beds and wardrobes, which were impossible to negotiate up the narrow stairs, to be brought in through the upstairs windows or, as one tenant remembered, being sawn in half!

The Susannah Place tenant list, compiled from official records, indicates that many of the 19th-century tenants moved frequently. They would have moved with only the bare necessities to furnish their homes. Yet most people owned small portable items such as ornaments and pictures and, as an 1881 newspaper article observed of houses in The Rocks, 'Flowers, pictures and knick-knacks were placed wherever an opportunity offered, and bore evidence of being carefully tended'.[12] As tenants, the residents of Susannah Place were not permitted to alter their dwelling structurally but within its walls they were free to create their own home.

For 90 years, from 1844 to 1935, the front room of No 64 operated as a grocer shop, which meant the tenants in this house had one less room for living. The first occupant of the shop was James Munro, a ginger beer maker, and it is possible that he manufactured ginger beer there. The bankruptcy file of George Hill, who ran the grocer shop from 1879 to 1898, gives us a rare insight into the types of goods sold in the late 1880s.[13] From the inventory of goods we can imagine the shelves with jars of coffee, tins of curry powder, nutmeg, baking powder, sardines and kippered herrings, bottles of lemonade and soda water, boxes of arrowroot biscuits, chocolate cremes and fancy biscuits, and below, crowded on the floor, would have been sacks of oatmeal, rice, potatoes, pearl barley, split peas and canary food. As Hill served customers, the shop would have filled with all manner of smells — the aromas of the tobacco, teas and cheese escaping each time he opened a tin or box to weigh the goods out.

It is unknown how the shop was fitted out in the 19th century but when James Young's parents ran it from 1904 to 1930,

Re-created c1915 shop window of Susannah Place Museum, 1991, photograph © Christopher Shain

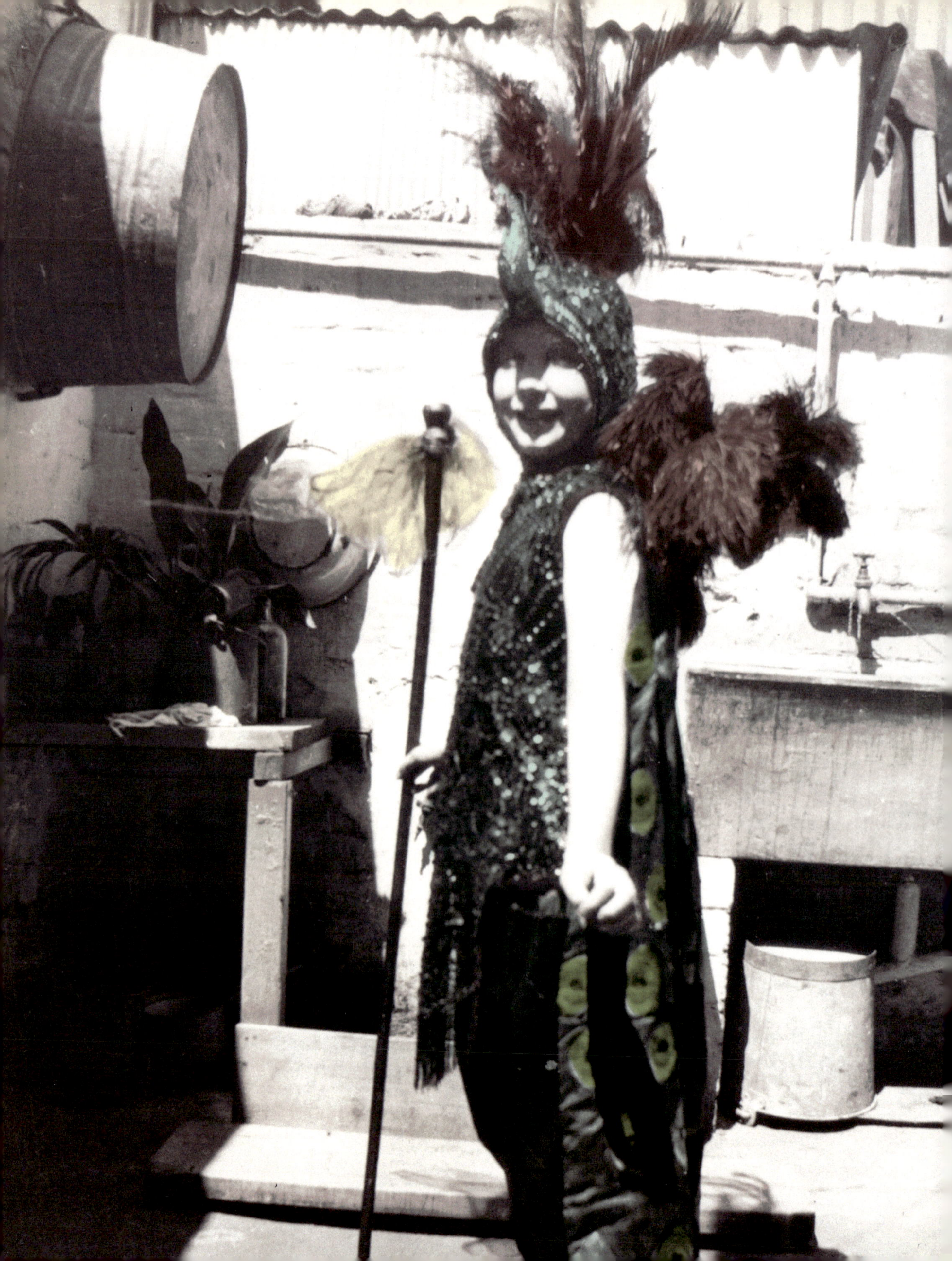

Sometimes we'd go swimming in the Domain baths and you'd have your bath there.[14]

Fred Hughes and Bertha Grayson, 1994. Tenants No 58 Gloucester St, 1915–31

This c1920s photograph is one of only a handful showing the backyards of Susannah Place. Behind Iris, who is posing in a magnificent peacock costume, can be seen the basic washing facilities for the Hughes family. Baths were taken in the round tin tub (hanging on the wall) set up in front of the fire in the basement kitchen. The hot water was boiled in the copper (just out of sight) and carried using the tin bucket. The laundry tubs were used for scrubbing clothes and washing the dishes. Next door at No 60 the Doyle family enjoyed more modern facilities; a corrugated iron washhouse had been built in their backyard.

Iris Hughes in the backyard of No 58 Gloucester Street, c1920s. Tenant No 58 Gloucester Street, 1915–31. Courtesy Cleo Grayson and Karen Moffatt

Mr G Hill

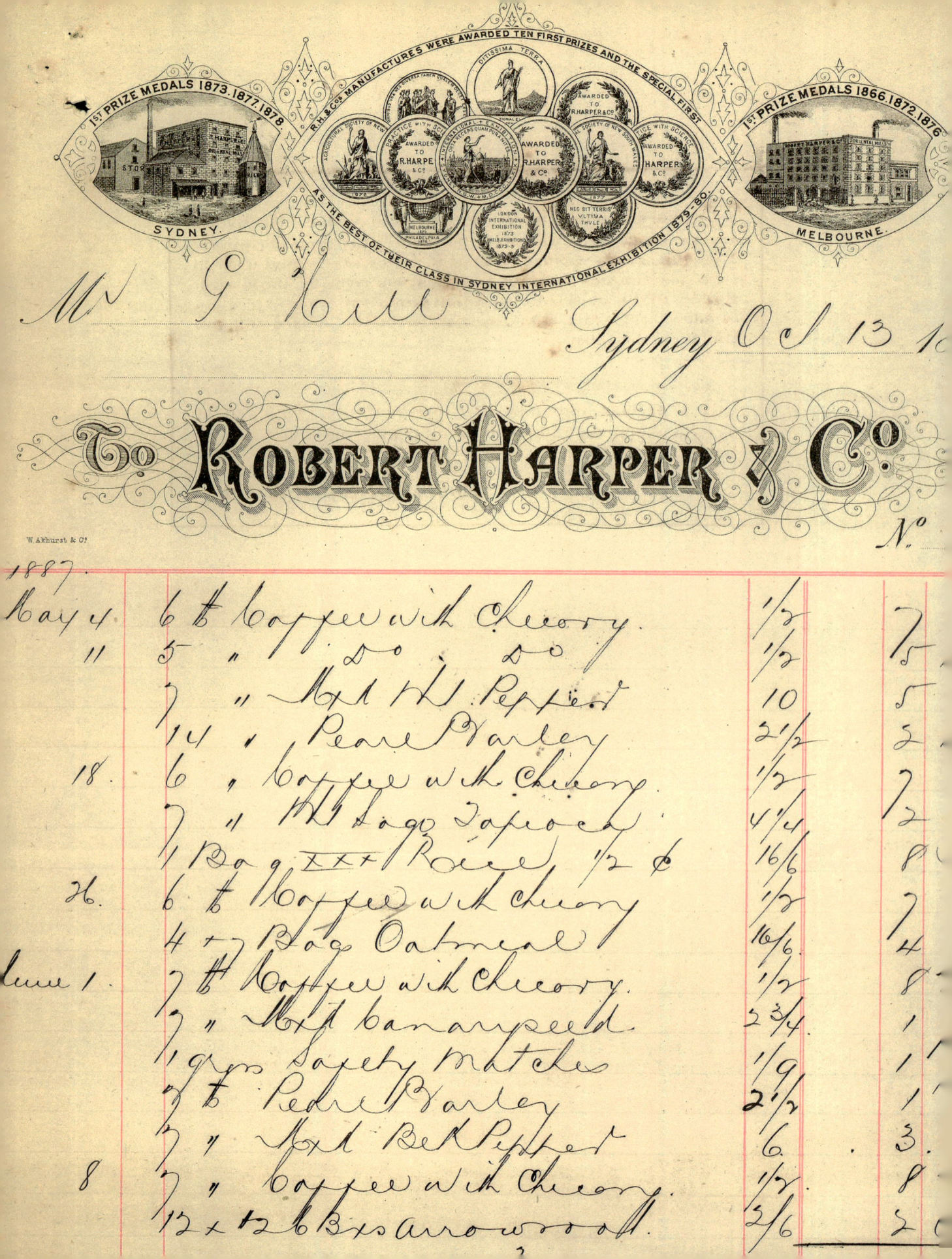

Sydney O/S 13 1[ ]

To Robert Harper & Co.

Nº

1887

May 4	6 ℔ Coffee with Chicory	1/2	7	
" 11	5 " Do Do	1/2	5	
	7 " Mxd Wt Pepper	10	5	
	14 " Pearl Barley	2½	2	
" 18	6 " Coffee with Chicory	1/2	7	
	7 " Wt Sago Tapioca	4¼	2	
	1 Bag XXX Rice ½ c	16/6	8	
" 26	6 ℔ Coffee with Chicory	1/2	7	
	½+7 Bag Oatmeal	16/6	4	
June 1	7 ℔ Coffee with Chicory	1/2	8	
	1/2 " Mxd Canaryseed	2¾	1	
	1 gross Safety Matches	1/9	1	
	9 ℔ Pearl Barley	2½	1	
	7 " Mxd Blk Pepper	6	3	
" 8	7 " Coffee with Chicory	1/2	8	
	12 + 12 ℔ Bxs Arrowroot	2/6	5	

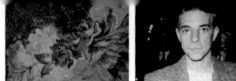

it is more than likely that the fittings had survived from earlier grocers. James remembers an L-shaped counter filling the small room with rows of shelves lining the walls behind. The two large windows facing the street and laneway were used to display goods to attract passing custom.

By 1935 the departure of shopkeepers Eliza and Robert Sneddon marked the end of retail trading from No 64. Some time later the shop fittings, including the counter and shelves, were removed and successive tenants used the shop space as a lounge room.

Behind the formal parlour were the rooms where 'ordinary living' occurred. Immediately behind, on the ground floor, was the dining room. However, by the early 20th century three of the houses had brought the kitchens upstairs, adding a fuel stove and later a gas stove to the room. Beryl Smith in No 64 and her neighbour Ellen Marshall at No 62 were still using their fuel stoves well into the 1960s, especially in the winter months. In No 58 there is no evidence of the back room ever being used as a kitchen and we know that for most of the 20th century it served as an additional bedroom. In the 1880s a small, enclosed timber verandah was added to the back rooms of Nos 62 and 64, which appears to have been used as additional kitchen space from at least the 1930s, and probably earlier, as a 'sleep-out'. In the 1950s Ron Smith fitted out his verandah at No 64 with a cupboard made out of an old kitchen cabinet and lined the walls with timber from the tea chests he had acquired while working at the Bushells Tea Factory. Ron or his wife Beryl had also laid at least three different patterned linoleums over the timber floor. An affordable and hard-wearing floor covering that came in myriad patterns and colours, linoleum

Eliza Sneddon, c1930s. Grocer and tenant No 64 Gloucester Street, 1931–35. Courtesy Janet Bubb **opposite** Goods supplied by Robert Harper and Co to grocer George Hill. Excerpt from George Hill's bankruptcy file, 1887, Supreme Court, Insolvency Files, State Records NSW

could be easily laid and maintained by the tenants, who when one layer began to show signs of wear, would simply place another sheet on top with a layer of newspaper in between. The front ground floor room of No 58 has five layers of floor coverings still in place, the first a c1900s floral-patterned oilcloth and the last a c1960s yellow and gold-flecked linoleum.

In 1891 there was an average of almost seven people to a house in The Rocks.[15] The sleeping arrangements in the two-bedroom houses must have been a constant challenge. How did 19th-century tenants like Mary and James Hill with their eight children, or Mary and Robert Bell with their seven, cope?

Some of the answers can be found in the stories of our 20th-century families. Describing the sleeping arrangements of his family of six, Fred Hughes, who lived in No 58 from 1915 to 1931, explains that he and his brother, Charles, slept upstairs in one room while parents Lena and Thomas slept downstairs in what should have been the dining room. His youngest sister, Iris, slept in a cot under the stairs, and another sister, Bertha, slept on a folding bed in the parlour. Despite these crowded arrangements, the family also took in lodgers, mostly fellow coal lumpers, who slept in the upstairs front bedroom.

It was common for families to take in boarders to help pay the rent during lean times. During World War II a Mrs Curtis boarded with John and Adelaide Gallagher in No 58 and had a little stove installed in her bedroom along with a wardrobe, dressing table, single bed and small table. In 1889 Eliza and Alfred Miller operated a boarding house in No 62, a venture in which Eliza's prior occupation as a domestic servant and Alfred's skills as a baker must have come in handy. We can only guess at how the house would have functioned. It is conceivable that more than four boarders at a time could have been accommodated with the parlour and dining room converted to bedrooms and meals taken in the basement kitchen.

Today's notions of privacy and personal space had no place in these houses in the 19th and early 20th centuries. Many of the internal doors were removed as they became difficult to close due to sagging ceilings. Children from the large families who lived at Susannah Place never knew the luxury of their own bedroom let alone their own bed. In the bedroom she shared with her two sisters, Patricia Thomas slept

Linoleum c1940s, No 60 Gloucester Street front room, ground floor, 2005, photograph © Ross Heathcote

… we had a double bed, a single bed and a small dressing table … and one wardrobe which wasn't very big but we didn't have much to fill it.[16]

Patricia Thomas, 1993. Tenant No 62 Gloucester Street, 1933–42

in a single bed while her sisters Colleen and Mercia shared a double bed. The eldest sister, Doreen, lived with a family friend above a cafe on George Street. In 1933 their brother, Ron, was born in the back bedroom and continued to share his parents' bedroom until he was nine.

Next door at No 58 there were five adults in the house by the time Florence and Leslie Gallagher moved in with Les's grandparents in 1944. To go down to the kitchen or the bathroom in the backyard they had to walk through his grandparents' bedroom.

The inherent dangers of gaslights meant they were rarely put upstairs in the bedrooms – most families used candles or kerosene lamps until electric lights were installed. Although the Australian Gas Light Company introduced gaslights to Sydney in 1841, they remained beyond the means of ordinary families until the introduction of penny-in-the-slot meters. From 1897 these meters, along with a pendant light and a gas ring for cooking, were installed for free.[17] The penny-in-the-slot meter allowed families who could not meet quarterly bills to pay as they went along; a penny lasted for about three hours.[18] It is still uncertain when gas came to Susannah Place. As Patricia recalls, it was important to have a ready supply of pennies:

The gas was run by the meter and we had to put a penny in the slot and we always had to have those pennies to put in the slot otherwise we'd have to sit in darkness and many times we'd be in the middle of a meal and all of a sudden the lights would all go out.[19]

The lack of electricity at No 58 was one of the reasons that drove the Hughes family to leave Susannah Place in 1931. Settling into their new electrically powered home in Millers Point, the family all 'thought they were kings!'[20] Although government authorities like the Maritime Services Board are remembered as benevolent landlords, improvements such as the construction of external washhouses or the installation of electricity were at their discretion and did not necessarily keep pace with those carried out in suburban households. As improvements often meant increased rents, poorer families waited until they could afford them, and as a result facilities at each of the houses were added at different times. No 64 (with the shop) was the first house to receive electricity in 1936, three years after the

Patricia Thomas in the re-created bedroom she shared with her two sisters in the 1940s at No 62 Gloucester Street, 2006, photograph © Christopher Shain

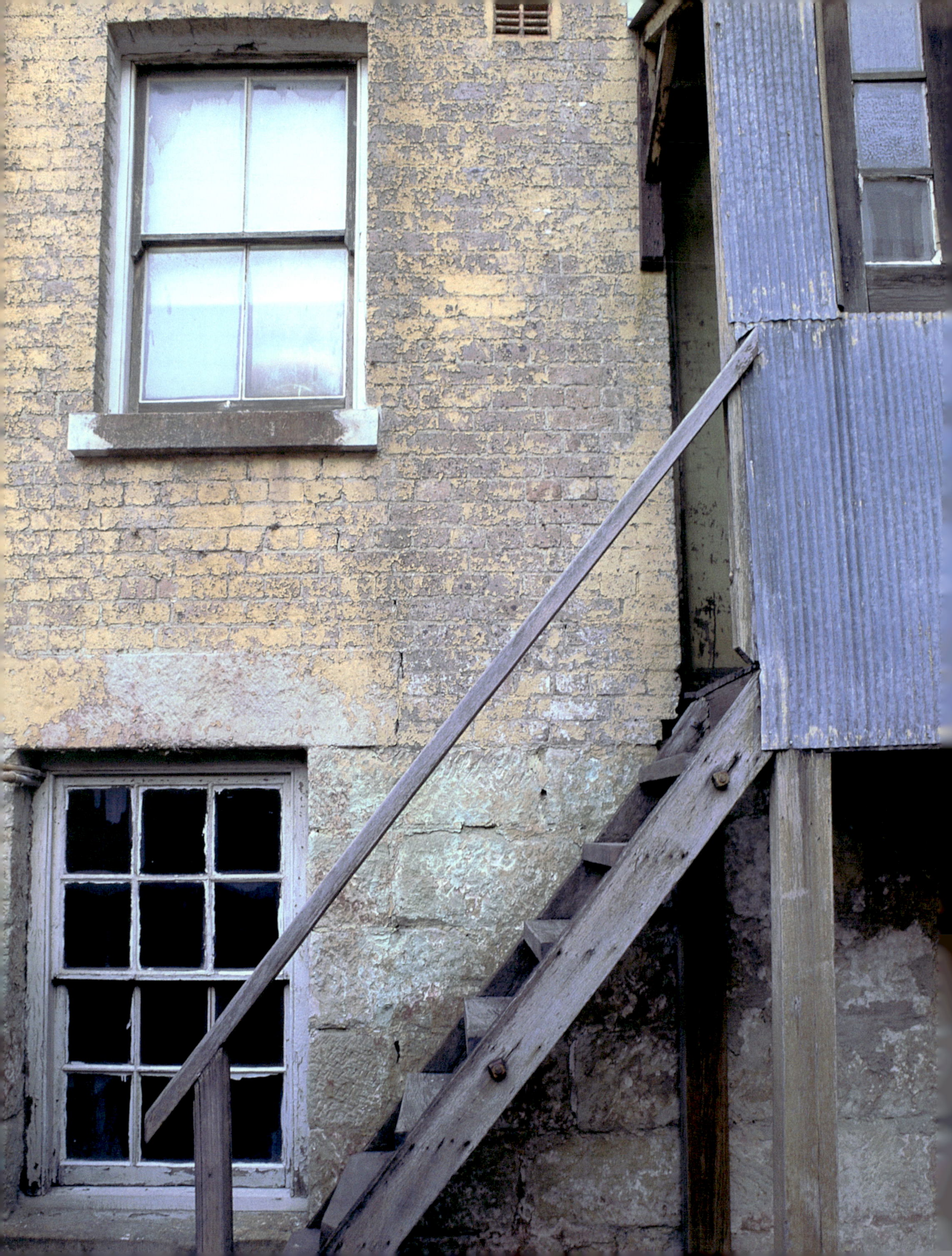

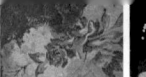

tenants requested it. Less fortunate were the Thompson family at No 62 who didn't get electric lights until 1942, the reason cited in a blunt entry on their tenant card: 'Board will not install electric light until rent arrears are paid'.[21]

From the back room a flight of timber stairs leads down into in the yard. Here, inside the original boundary walls (the yards of Nos 58, 60 and 62 were extended), are the toilet and washing facilities. Simple corrugated iron washhouses, with tin baths, were added to three of the houses between 1910 and 1930 and one was still in use until the mid 1970s. Hot water from the copper was originally carried to the bath by buckets – a ritual the Andersen family called the 'bucket brigade'.[22] No 62 never had a washroom built and up until the late 1960s the Marshalls were still filling the tin bath located under the window in the basement with hot water from the copper. Before the washhouses were built baths were taken in a tin tub in front of the fuel stove in the kitchen, though Fred Hughes remembers being bathed in the copper. Access to these external facilities as well as to the basement kitchens was difficult when it rained and no doubt hazardous when trying to negotiate the steep stairs with a basket full of washing or a chamber pot that needed emptying. Over the years, successive tenants erected canvas awnings as well as makeshift corrugated iron roofs over the stairs and yards. All that remains today are an assortment of hooks and pulleys and the outline of a roof that once covered the entrance to the basement of No 58.

The basement kitchen of No 58 was in continuous operation from 1844 to 1974. Today the room still retains evidence

Mary 'Girlie' Andersen in No 58 Gloucester Street basement kitchen, c1950s. Tenant No 58, 1949–64. Courtesy Jack Andersen **opposite**
Rear stairs, No 58 Gloucester Street, 1998, photograph Richard Gange. Susannah Place Museum Collection, Historic Houses Trust

of nearly 150 years of use; the original 1840s 12-pane window is intact, countless layers of linoleum dating from the 1920s cover the dirt floor, the 1950s green and yellow paint scheme survives, and the gas pipes and electric wiring charting the introduction of modern services to the kitchen can still be seen.

Remarkably, a photograph (opposite) of this room taken in the 1920s captures the everyday details of the Hughes family kitchen with its pots and pans, fuel stove and kitchen sink. Fred Hughes's memories were recorded in the 1990s and his words evoke the cooking smells that once filled this room: 'We had a lot of fish soup. Father would bring home fish he used to catch. There was always fish simmering in a pot on the stove'.[23]

During the plague-cleansing operations of the early 20th century houses and lives were inspected, carbolic solution swilled down drains and toilets, rubbish removed and lime wash painted on the interiors and exteriors of buildings. The lath and plaster ceilings in the basements of Susannah Place were stripped out and the rooms given a coat of lime wash, the remnants of which survive today. It is not known why Nos 60, 62 and 64 abandoned the use of their basement kitchens. It may have been prompted by the inconvenience of going outside in all weather to get to the kitchen and then having to carry the food upstairs to eat.

During World War II the Andersen family obtained permission to use the basement of No 64 as an air-raid shelter. Girlie Andersen fitted out the room with tinned food and Martin Andersen, in his role as air-raid warden, made sure that neighbours were inside when the siren sounded. In the 1950s, when the Smiths were tenants, the basement was used for less noble purposes; an 'SP bookie' (an illegal bookmaker) operated out of the space on Saturday afternoons, paying the tenants £5 per week for the privilege! The Smiths also used the room as an additional bedroom to accommodate their visiting relatives.

The cellars had a small grate opening to Gloucester Street where coal was dropped through to the floor below. In No 64 the cellar was also used to store foodstuffs from the grocer shop above. To protect the stock from vermin Hugo Youngein would keep goods like sugar in a tin-lined piano case. When the shop ceased trading and coal was no longer

Fred Hughes in No 58 Gloucester Street basement kitchen, c1920s. Tenant No 58, 1915–31. Courtesy Cleo Grayson and Karen Moffatt

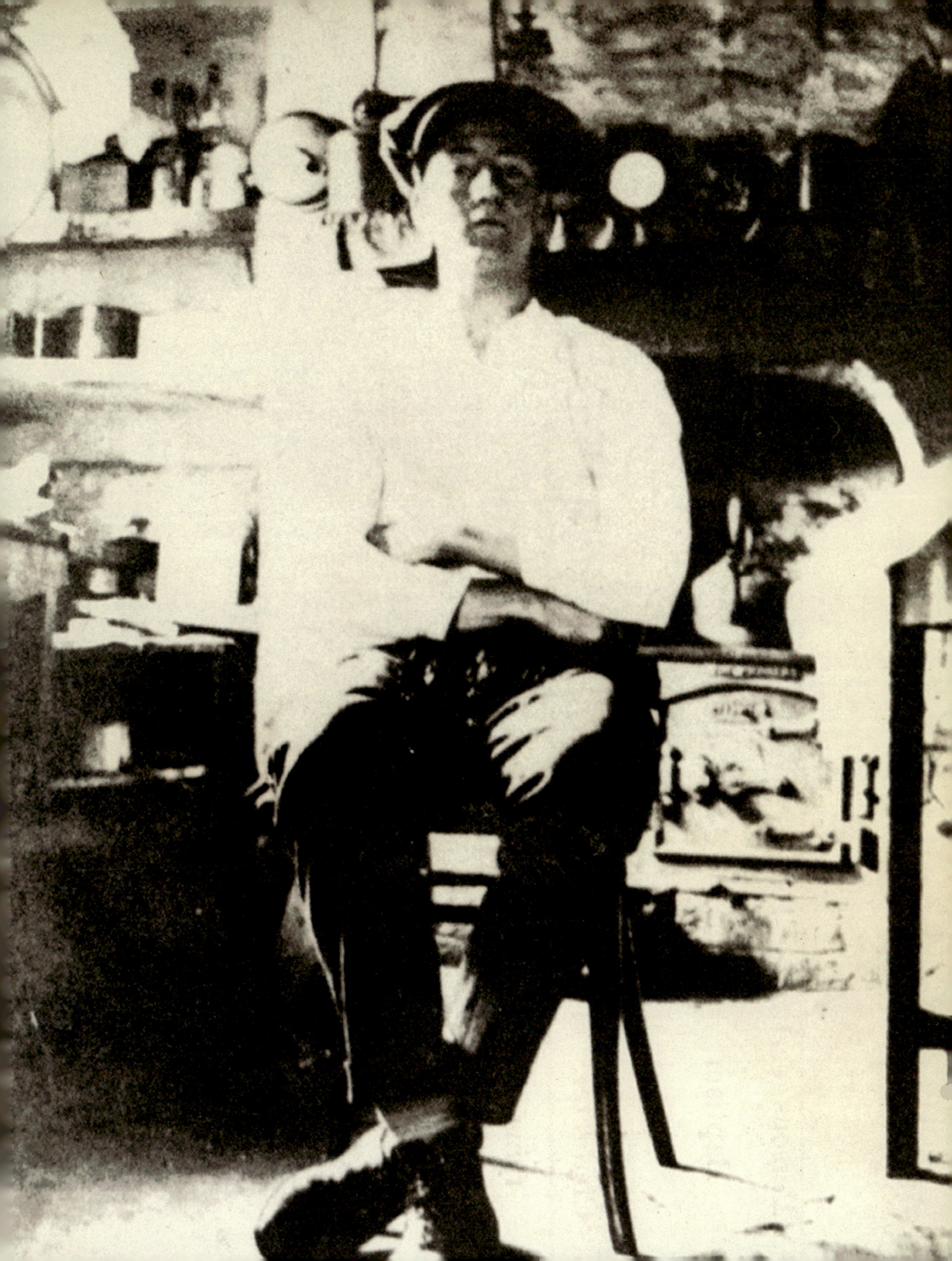

needed for the fuel stoves, the cellars were filled with pieces of old furniture, tools, bicycles and scooters and numerous other disused household objects.

Despite the limited space, gardens were established on the sandstone ledge that ran through the entire length of the backyards. Small garden beds were fashioned out of bricks; with vegetables, flowers and herbs grown with varying degrees of success. Patricia Thomas's stepfather grew all the things she disliked – 'spinach, chokos and beans' – and she was given the 'terribly embarrassing job' of collecting manure from the streets for the garden.[24] Some of the tenants kept chickens in wire coops ready for Christmas and many had pets. With so much going on in these tiny yards, there was little space for children to play and, inevitably, the backyards soon spilled into the nearby streets and lanes.

Up until the late 1960s the houses in The Rocks, including Susannah Place, were well maintained by the Maritime Services Board and its tenants. However, with the announcement of redevelopment plans for the area by the newly formed Sydney Cove Redevelopment Authority the routine maintenance for houses declined – roofs were left to leak and termites went unchecked – as part of a deliberate strategy to encourage people to move out. Ellen Marshall described what she saw happening in the area as 'demolition by neglect'.[25] By 1974, three of the Susannah Place houses were empty and the Marshalls in No 62 became the unofficial caretakers of the entire terrace. They made repairs at their own expense, maintained the gardens and hung curtains in the windows to deter vandals and squatters. But despite their best efforts, the vacant houses were to suffer the effects of over ten years of neglect. Today this damage forms part of the history of the houses and has been left as a reminder of those times.

Adelaide (Ada) Gallagher with grandsons, Ernie and Jack Andersen, in the backyard of No 58 Gloucester Street, c1940s. Tenant No 58, 1934–49. Courtesy Ernie Andersen.

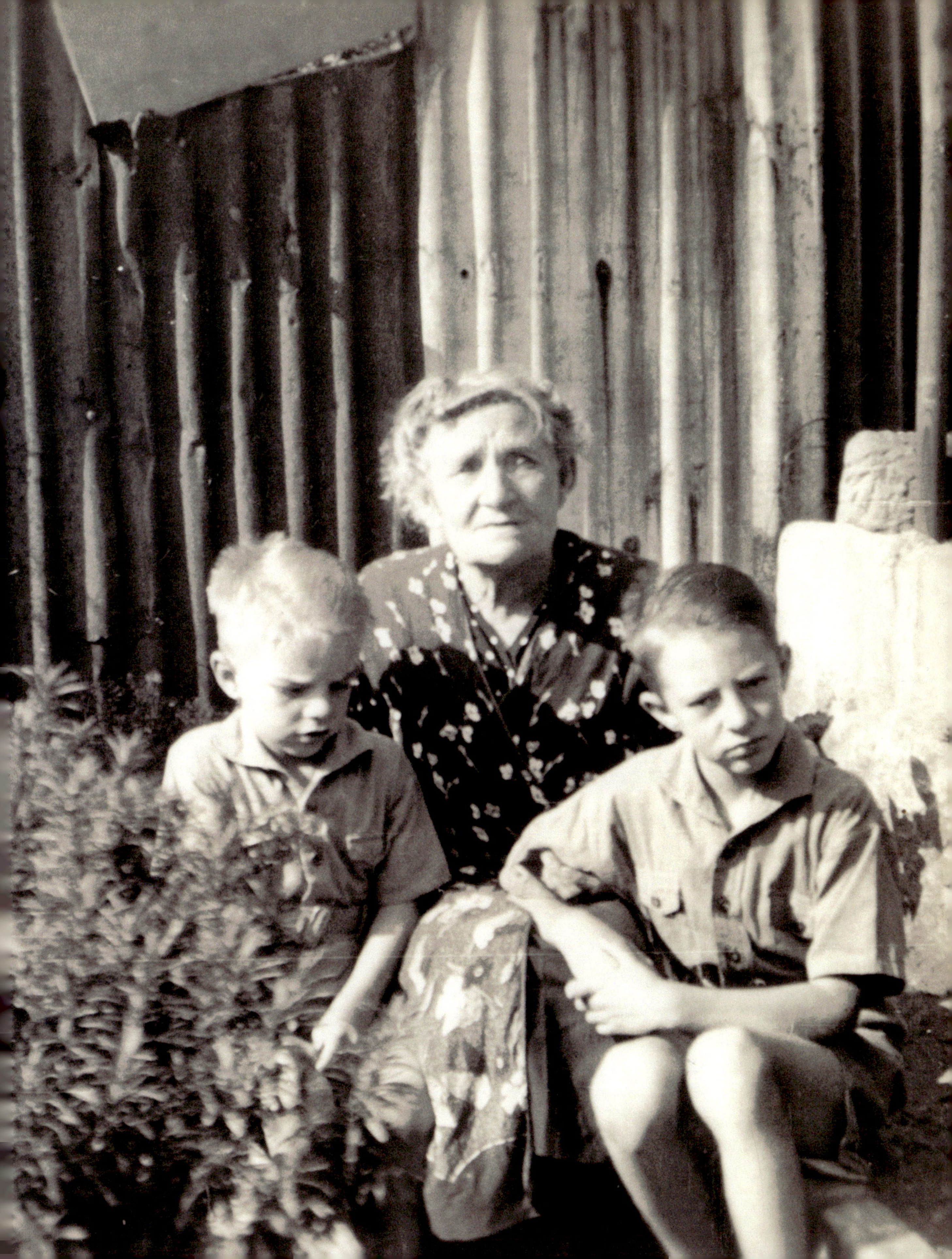

MAKING A MARK

108 Close-up details of Susannah Place, 2004, photographs © Ross Heathcote

Close-up details of Susannah Place, 2004, photographs © Ross Heathcote

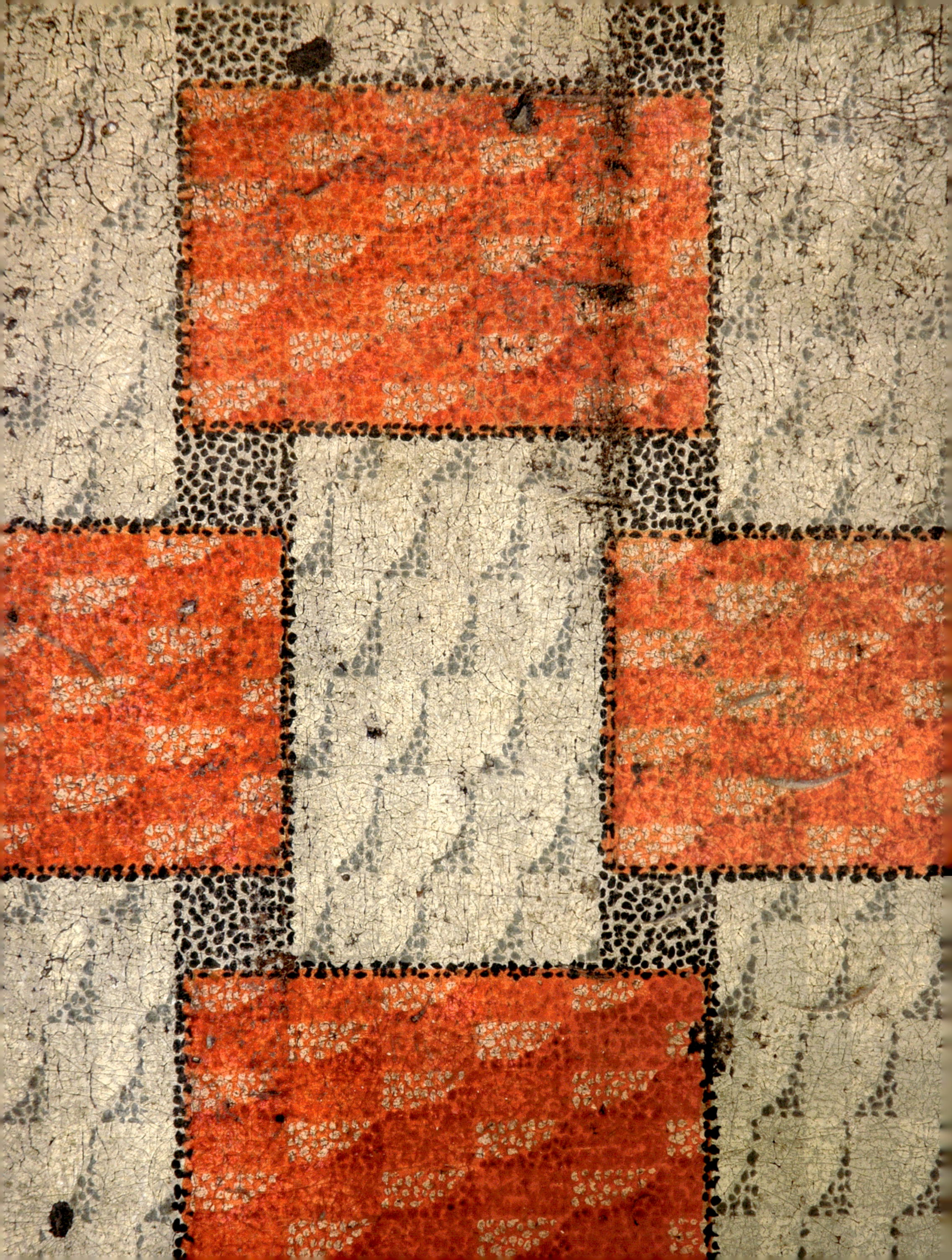

MAKING A MARK

1. Lionel Brett, *The things we see: houses*, Penguin Books, Middlesex, 1947, p3.
2. Peter Emmett, '*They didn't have any locks on their doors like you have to have now*', Susannah Place – The Rocks: a working-class neighbourhood, unpublished report, Historic Houses Trust, Sydney, 1989, p13.
3. William Stanley Jevons, 'Remarks upon the social map of Sydney, 1858', manuscript, Microfilm CY 1045, Mitchell Library, State Library of New South Wales, p34.
4. Stefan Muthesius, *The English terraced house*, Yale University Press, New Haven and London, 1982, p46.
5. George Adaley and Kay Kallas oral history, 1993.
6. Jack and Shirly Andersen oral history, 1992.
7. Leslie and Florence Gallagher oral history, 1992.
8. Ellen Marshall and Jenni Whitford oral history, 1993.
9. Patricia Thomas (nee O'Brien/Thompson) oral history, 1993.
10. William Stanley Jevons, 'Remarks upon the social map of Sydney, 1858', p34.
11. James Young (Youngein) oral history, 1990.
12. *Sydney Morning Herald*, 7 January 1881.
13. Supreme Court, Insolvency files 1842–87, File No 22403. CGS 13654, State Records NSW.
14. Fred Hughes and Bertha Grayson (nee Hughes) oral history, 1994.
15. Max Kelly (ed), *Nineteenth century Sydney: essays in urban history*, Sydney University Press, Sydney, 1978, p71.
16. Patricia Thomas oral history, 1993.
17. Rosemary Broomham, *First light: 150 years of gas*, Hale & Iremonger, Sydney, 1987, p92.
18. ibid
19. Patricia Thomas oral history, 1993.
20. Fred Hughes oral history, 1992.
21. Tenant card file No 62 Gloucester Street, Sydney Harbour Foreshore Authority.
22. Ernie Andersen oral history, 1990.
23. Fred Hughes and Bertha Grayson oral history, 1994.
24. Patricia Thomas oral history, 1993.
25. Ellen Marshall and Jenni Whitford oral history, 1993.

left Corrugated iron wall, No 64 Gloucester Street, 2004, photograph © Ross Heathcote **centre** Linoleum c1960. No 60 Gloucester Street kitchen, 2004, photograph © Ross Heathcote **right** Jeffrey and Kristine Smith. Tenants No 64 Gloucester Street, 1956–72. Courtesy Ron Smith **opposite** Linoleum c1960, No 60 Gloucester Street kitchen, 2004, photograph © Ross Heathcote

Houses are parts of people and people are parts of houses.[1]
Sali Herman, 1958

SHARED

5

HISTORY
SEPARATE LIVES

Oral history gives history back to the people in their own words. It allows heroes not just from the leaders, but from the unknown majority of the people.[2]

Paul Thompson, 1978

As artist Sali Herman observed, the intertwined relationships and destinies of houses and people are difficult to separate. The voices of Susannah Place's 19th-century residents are harder to hear as they left behind few personal records or belongings. Official documents such as birth, marriage and death certificates allow us to follow the progress of their lives, and the archaeology of these and neighbouring houses gives us an insight into their everyday belongings. But we will never know all their names or the names of the tenants and lodgers who came after them, much less the stories of their lives.

The residents of Susannah Place led ordinary lives in sometimes extraordinary times – they raised families, worked, shopped, dreamed and suffered disappointments, watched the Harbour Bridge being built and witnessed the destruction of their community. Their elusive stories are also our stories and in them we can hear echoes of our own family histories.

With some coaxing, the former tenants of Susannah Place have generously allowed us into their lives. Most were bemused that we should want to hear their story, believing it to be 'nothing special'. Yet it is this very ordinariness that resonates with visitors from around the world. As one resident, Flo Gallagher, said of the oral histories, 'the voice'll put the colour in it. The story is just plain black and white print, isn't it?'[3]

The story of Susannah Place is of a shared history of four houses that existed side by side and the people who lived in them. As neighbours, they couldn't help but hear the footsteps on the stairs, the rows between husbands and wives, the conversations in the yards or the back-to-back toilets being flushed. They could smell what they each cooked for dinner and they invariably caught sight of each other on the back stairs or over the shared fences. Yet despite living such similar lives, they rarely went into each other's homes.

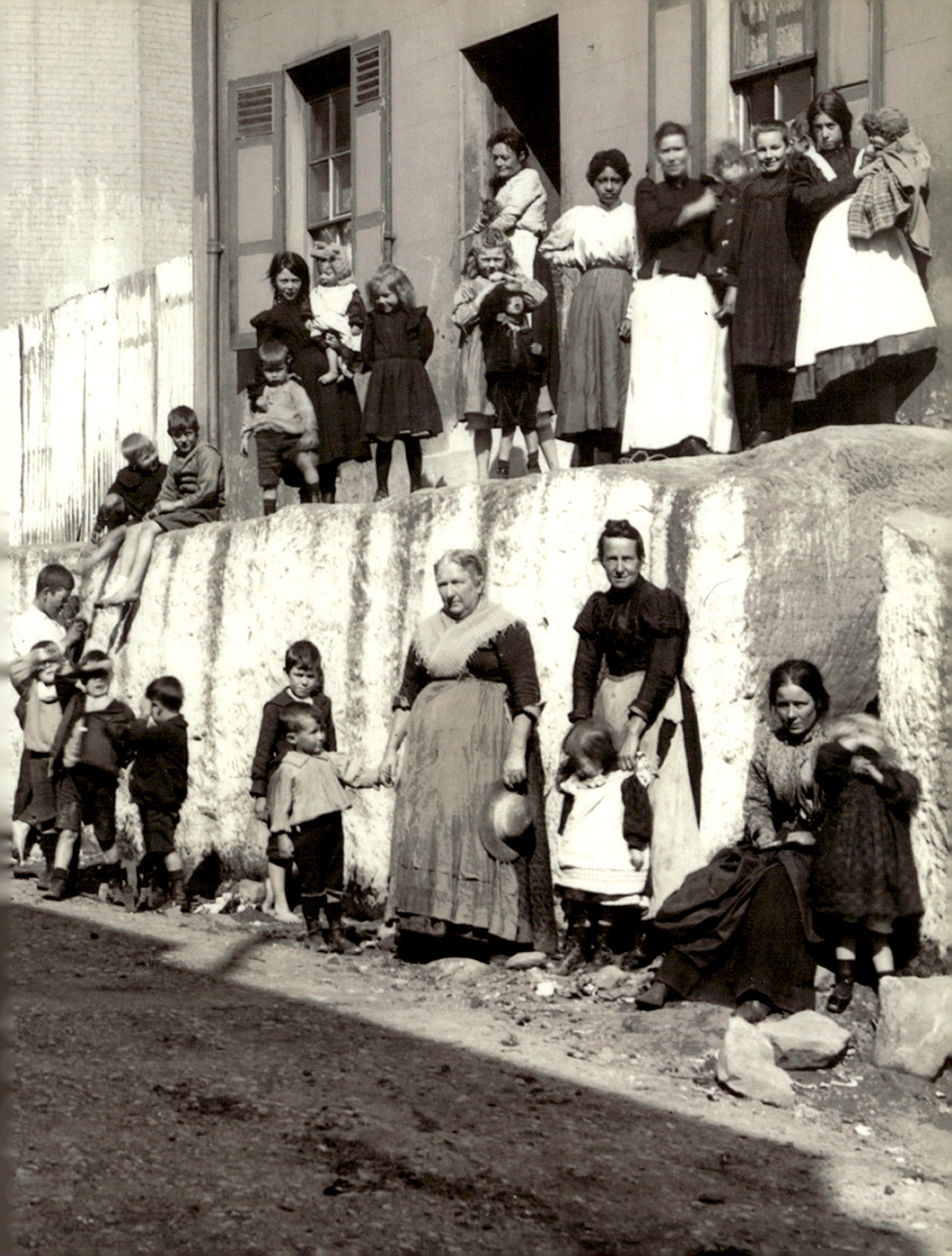

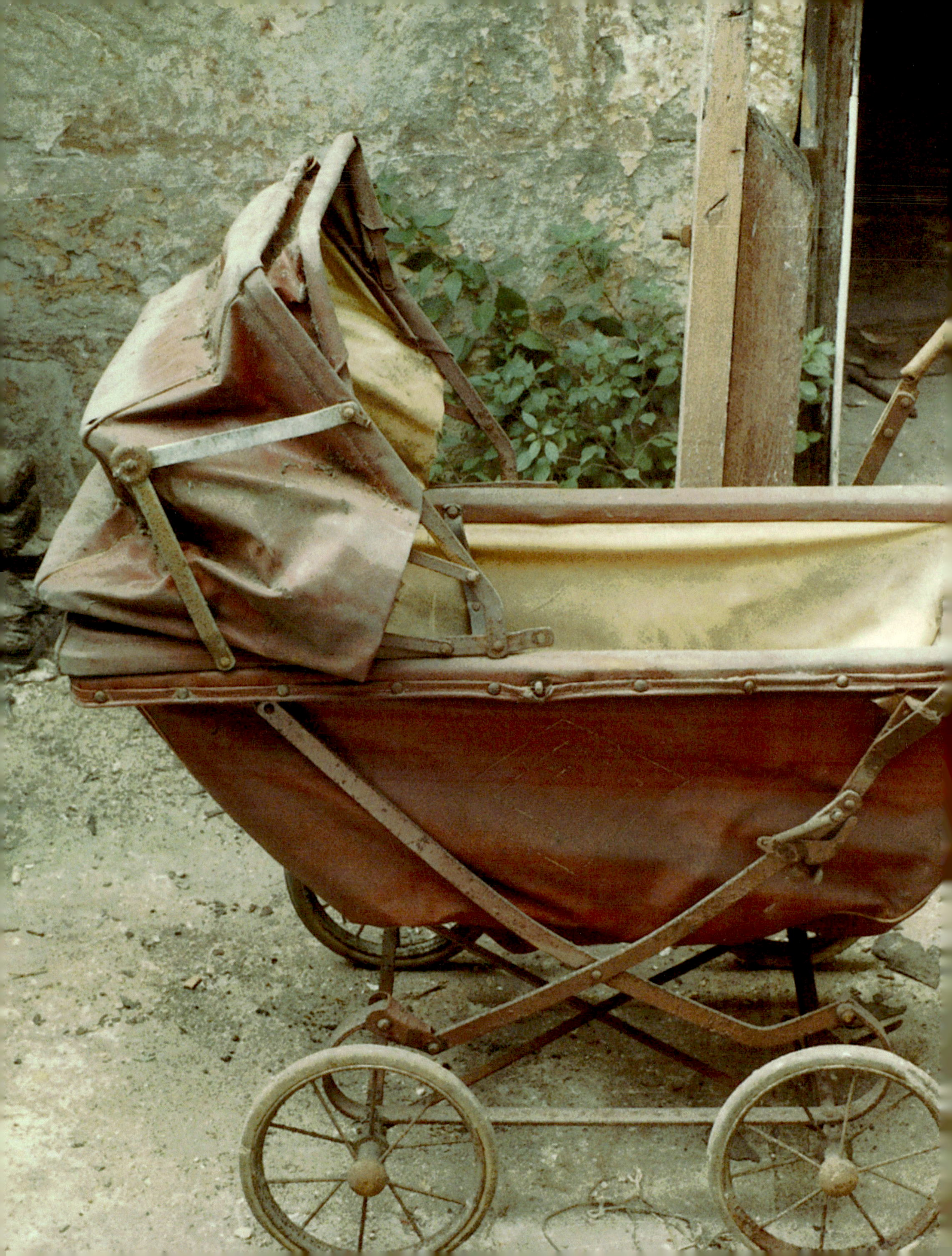

Former resident Jack Andersen considered his mother Girlie to be the 'best gossip' in the street. She knew all her neighbours but rarely ventured into their homes: 'She'd speak to them from outside. No one went in to have cups of tea'.[4]

An exception to this unwritten code was when women assisted each other with the birth of a child. In 1933 Margaret Thompson gave birth to her fifth child, Ronald, in the upstairs back bedroom of No 62. Her daughter Patricia described the scene of the birth: 'Nurse Martin was there and about half a dozen neighbours the night my brother was born'.[5] Nurse Martin was the local midwife who Fred Hughes recalls 'brought all the babies to life round here', including his youngest sister, born in No 58.[6]

Research into 15 of the 19th-century women who had lived at Susannah Place reveals that they gave birth to an average of six children. Between the ages of 19 and 36, Mary Rule, resident of No 58 from 1873 to 1886, gave birth to 11 children, of whom only three survived beyond infancy. In 1877 Bridget Merchant, at age 43, gave birth to her eighth and last child, Walter. The Merchants were well known in Gloucester Street. William Thomas Merchant had been the publican of the Whalers Arms Hotel, and had previously run boarding houses in the area.[7] The Merchants moved into No 60, just across the road from the hotel, in 1875 after being declared bankrupt. William attributed his insolvency to 'lapses of business and dullness of trade' and to 'the expenses incidental to the maintenance of a numerous family'.[8]

Despite the setback William is listed as bank manager on Walter's birth certificate. In 1878, a year after Walter's birth, the Merchants' 18-year-old daughter, Mary Jane, married Robert Bell, a cook. The couple lived with Mary's parents and after William's death took over the lease of No 60, where four of their ten children were born. Bridget had meanwhile moved further south along Gloucester Street to open a grocer shop.

From the mid 1830s immigrants from Britain took advantage of the government's 'Bounty Immigration' scheme to start a new life in the colony. Funded by the sale of land in the colony, the scheme was designed to encourage the immigration of skilled agricultural workers and tradesmen, and their families. The government funded the passage of the

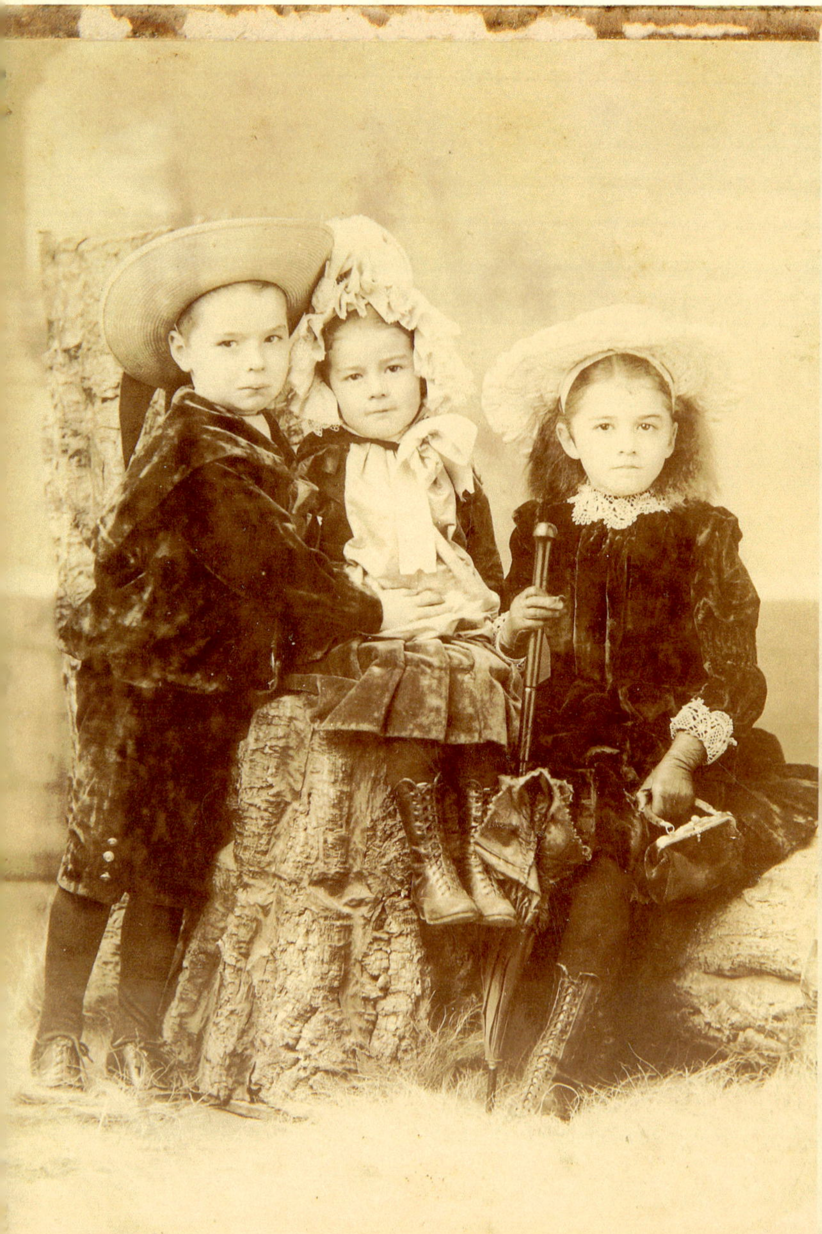

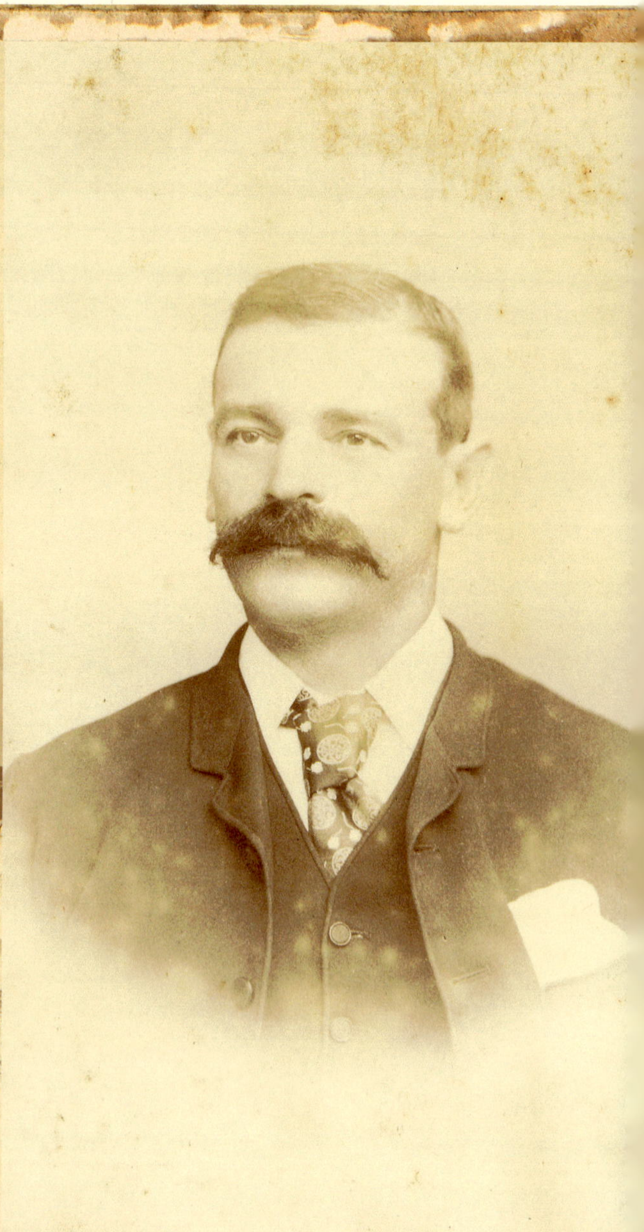

> *Sydney resembles very much an English seaport-town and you are reminded at every step of the strictly British character of the inhabitants …*[9]

Samuel Mossman and Thomas Banister, 1853

immigrants, and the emigration agents who were responsible for signing them up were paid a 'bounty' per person. Advertisements such as the following in the *West Briton* were placed in newspapers across Britain.

> EMIGRATION TO AUSTRALIA — A FINE first-class SHIP, of 500 Tons burthen, with … very superior accommodations for Cabin, Intermediate, and Steerage Passengers, will be dispatched … from the RIVER THAMES, direct for Sydney … A very extensive demand exists in this Colony for married Mechanics, particularly Carpenters, Joiners, Stone-masons, Stone-cutters, Bricklayers … also for Agricultural Servants, Shepherds … and Gardeners. …[10]

In 1840 Ellen and Francis Cunninghame, with their three young children and Ellen's sister, arrived in Sydney as assisted immigrants. Francis was an Irish-born printer working in Glasgow when he answered an advertisement calling for skilled compositors in Sydney. In 1844 the Cunninghames became No 60's first tenants. During their two years in the house, Ellen gave birth to a daughter, also named Ellen.

The Rocks continued to attract immigrants from around the world long after the immigration scheme ceased. The majority of Susannah Place's earliest tenants were immigrants, many of them sailors like Swedish seaman Hugo Lyunggren (anglicised to Youngein) who jumped ship in 1887, never to return home. Youngein worked in The Rocks as a coal lumper where he met and married Clara Thomas, a housemaid at the Australian Hotel. The couple ran the corner grocer's shop in No 64 from 1904 to 1930.

Similar stories emerge of other residents. Although Thomas Hughes never spoke much about his life in Liverpool, his son recalls 'he shot through by 11 or 12' and became a cabin boy on a sailing ship.[11]

George Lindon and his children (left to right) George Francis, Martha Georgina and Mary Gertrude, c1890s. Tenants No 58 Gloucester Street, 1887–99. Courtesy John Lindon Smee

Dear Mother and Father ... I am glad to say we have got to our journey's end safe and well, we reached Sydney on the Sunday ... I must tell you we had a very good voyage, but tiring, I think I shall like Sydney very much. It is a fine place. The buildings here are very large. It is the depth of winter here now but it is like the summer at home. The sun is shining and is quite warm. I think it warm now but they all think it cold ...[12]

Lizzie Sayce, 1901, tenant No 60 Gloucester Street, 1909–10

In 1901, after a long voyage from London, George and Mary 'Lizzie' Sayce arrived in Sydney with their young son. Lizzie's letter to her parents in August of that year was probably typical of many immigrants' reactions to their new home.

Lizzie and George Sayce with their children Marjorie and George, c1911. Tenants No 60 Gloucester Street, 1909–10. Courtesy Jean Ritchie

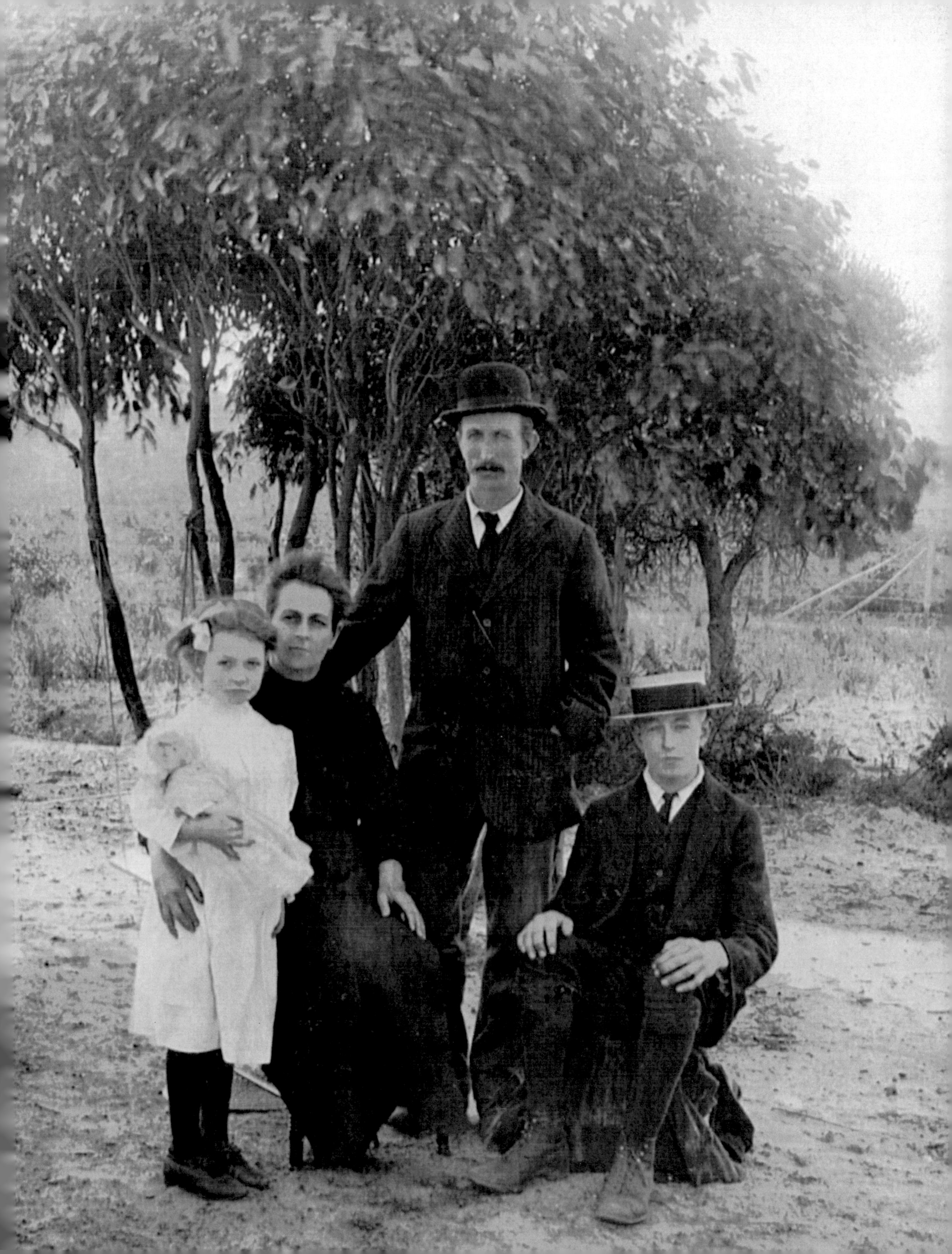

Form B

3.

COMMONWEALTH OF AUSTRALIA

STATUTORY DECLARATION
Referred to in Paragraph 1 of annexed Application.

1. Name in full. (Write clearly) I, Emmanuel Sarandedes

do solemnly and sincerely declare that—

1. My name is Emmanuel Sarandedes

2. My place of residence is at 60 Gloucester Street, Sya
in the State of N.S.W.

3. My personal description is as follows:—
Age 53 years   Height 5' 5"
Colour of Hair Brown   Colour of Eyes Brown
Any special Peculiarities Birth Mark on Right Cheek

4. My occupation is Cook in which capacity
I am at present and have been employed by Phillips & Protos
at 379 Pitt Street, Sydn
for a period of nine years

2. Name and address of employer.

3. Name of city, town, or locality.

5. I was born on the 15th day of September in the year 1891, at Cania in the Crete
in the country of Greece

4. Country, State, Department, Province, or as the case may be.

6. My nationality is Greek
The nationality of my father was Greek
His full name was Sarandis Sarandedes
The nationality of my mother prior to her marriage was Greek

5. French, Italian, or as the case may be.

7. I arrived in Australia from Crete
on the 1st day of May in the year 1914
per the Hamburg and disembarked at the port
of Sydney

6. Name of ship.

7. State places and periods in each.

8. Since my arrival in Australia I have resided at Sydney, 30 years

It is believed he jumped ship in Western Australia, eventually finding his way to The Rocks where he worked as a coal lumper and raised his family. Arnt Martinius Andersen from Oslo, Norway, also jumped ship, and later married a local woman, Mary Pauline Gallagher, with whom he raised two sons.

Little was known about the Sarantides family beyond the electoral rolls, fragments of a 1946 Greek newspaper found under a layer of linoleum and olive seeds found in the kitchen hearth, until Dorothea's grandchildren, Kay and George, visited Susannah Place Museum over 50 years later. Kay's recollections of their weekly visits to 'Nan' brought these small traces and bare facts to life:

> *I would have been ten or eleven and George about eight and we'd come and visit our grandmother and try to do a few little odd jobs for her – empty the chamber pot, a little bit of scrubbing of the floors, mop upstairs. There was a gas ring on the stove and I would put the iron to heat and do the shirts. I ironed on the table with a blanket over it …* [13]

Emmanuel and Arthur Sarantides had emigrated from Crete in 1914. Arthur went to Brisbane and worked as a hairdresser while his brother Emmanuel ran the Colonial Cafe at 139 George Street, The Rocks. In 1923 Emmanuel brought his mother and sister to Australia and later, two more brothers. The family lived above the cafe until 1935 when Emmanuel, Arthur and their mother, Dorothea, moved into 60 Gloucester Street where they lived until 1946. Their neighbours remember Dorothea as an old woman who couldn't speak much English and would occasionally pass some Greek food she had cooked over the fence to them. During World War II Emmanuel, Arthur and Dorothea, like many thousands of

Dorothea 'Rose' Sarantides, c1930s. Tenant No 60 Gloucester Street, 1936–46. Courtesy Kay Kallas **opposite** The Sarantides family name is spelt various ways on official documents – Sarandides, Sarandedes and Sarandithis. Emmanuel Sarandedes, Application for Certificate of Naturalization 1944, National Archives of Australia

The population of the 'Rocks' is largely composed of those who work in connection with shipping making it imperative that they should live in this neighbourhood.[14]

City Improvement Advisory Board, 1902–03

people not born in Australia or the United Kingdom, were required to register as 'aliens'. Their photos were taken and attached to the forms; Dorothea's age exempted her from being fingerprinted.

Lives in the hardy waterside community were in tune with the ebbs and flows of the harbour. A large proportion of Rocks men worked on the waterfront, 'on the coals' (coal lumpers) or on wharves (wharfies). Evidence taken for the 1859 Select Committee on the Condition of the Working Classes described how men were 'busily employed' during the wool season but at other times were 'hanging out on the corners of busy streets looking out for a day's or hour's job; and their wives [took] in washing to support their husbands and families'.[15]

The 1917 tram strike that spread to the waterfront had a profound effect on the area. It dragged on for months and saw hundreds of wharf workers' families struggling to survive. Thomas Hughes of No 58, a coal lumper, was unemployed with a wife and four children to support. During the strike his son Fred, aged 13, was given special permission to finish school and start work. Fred's first job was a paper-run in front of Customs House. He is recorded as saying, 'What money I could, I'd give my mother ... I was earning more than my father in the finish'.[16]

Fred's mother, Lena, went back to work waitressing while Thomas gambled what little they had to support the family. The Youngeins who lived next door were insulated from the immediate impact of the strike; their small grocer shop at Susannah Place continued to trade and extended credit to its regular customers who were unable to pay.

For some families the pressures of everyday life took its toll. Patricia Thomas remembers her stepfather, James 'Perc' Thompson, ruling 'with an iron hand'.

Wharfies, Circular Quay, 1910, Harold Cazneaux. Reproduced courtesy Cazneaux family and National Library of Australia **overleaf**
Children sitting on the Cumberland Place steps with James Youngein (Young) top row, far right, c1915. Courtesy Young family

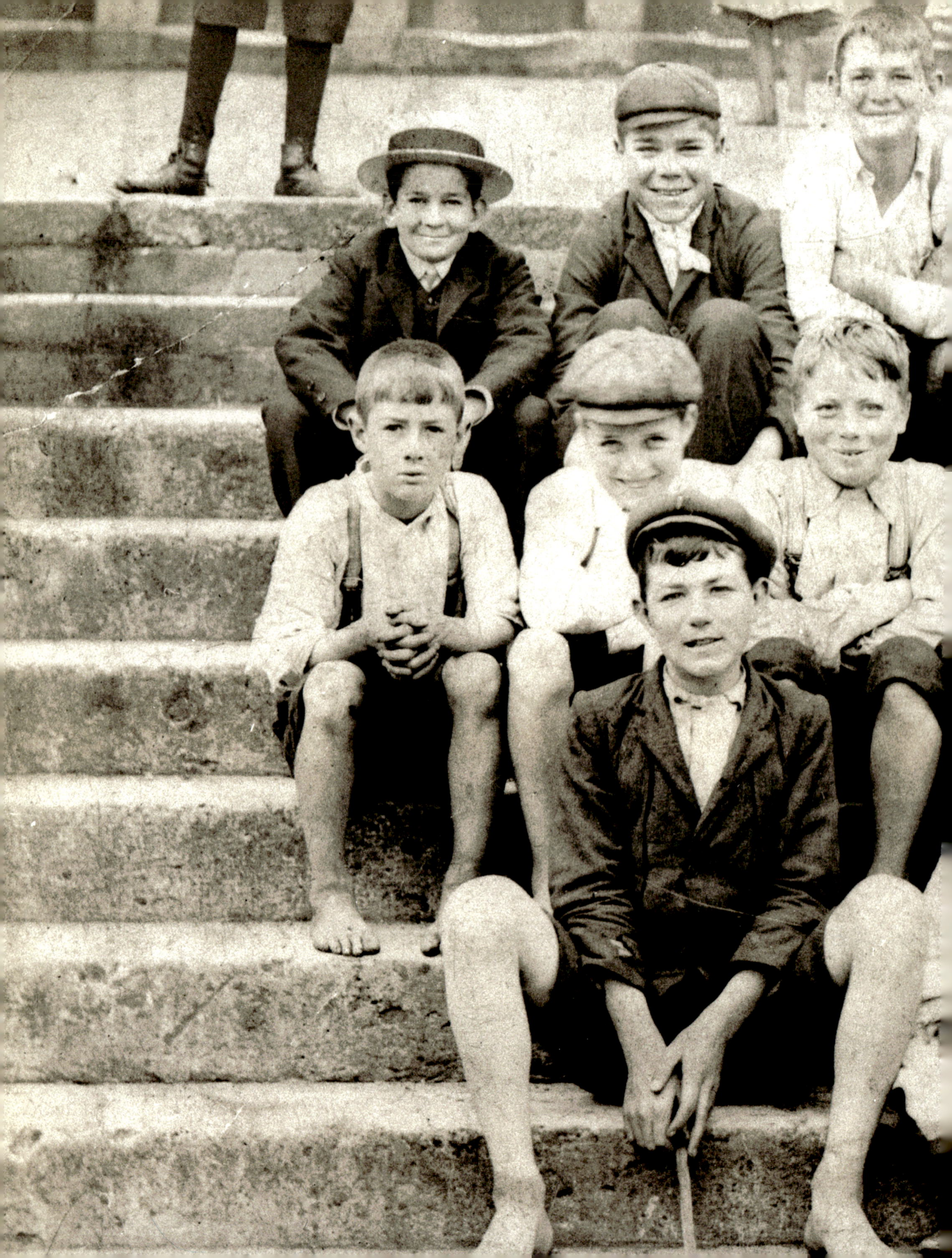

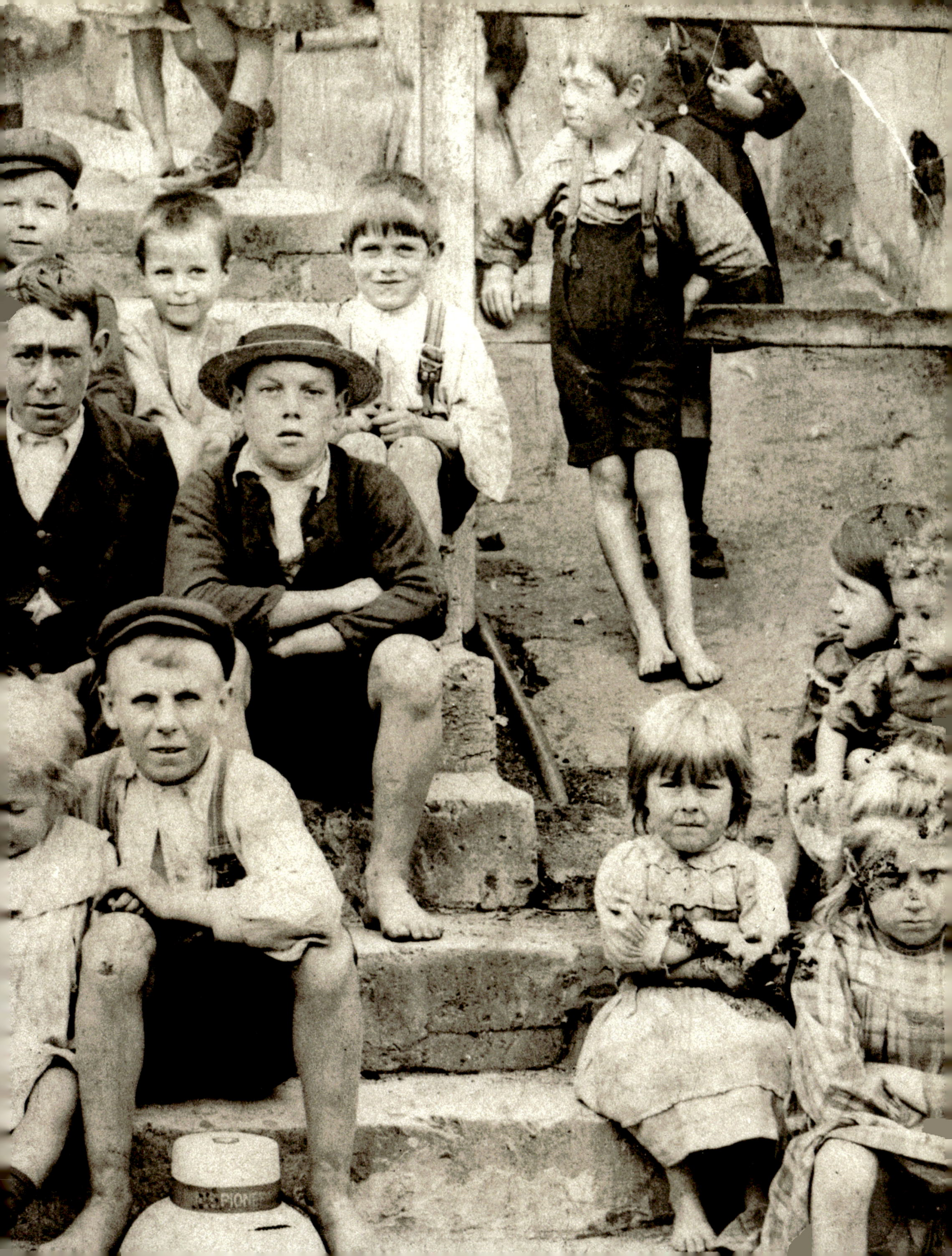

Perc was in and out of work during the Depression years and began drinking too much: 'My mother took a blanket over to the hotel ... and threw it in the bar and told him "you're here all the time you might as well sleep here"'.[17] Finally, one day in 1942, after nine years together, Margaret packed up her children and left Perc and her home at No 62. Perc's son Ron continued to visit and stay with his father and can recall being both 'the apple of his father's eye' and the target of his violent temper.[18]

Domestic violence was a familiar theme in many families, often compounded by poverty and unemployment. Annie Poynter's move to No 60 was one of many to keep ahead of her alcoholic and violent husband. Annie and her youngest son, Leslie, lived with close friend Elizabeth McRitchie at No 60 while her two elder sons lived with their grandfather. Leslie Poynter recalls a childhood marked by instability and fear: 'As a young child, we all witnessed a lot of this and it wasn't pleasant ... children running out of the place screaming, voices raised and punches going ...'[19]

The Depression years of the 1930s were extremely tough on workers. Fred Hughes remembers the gruelling hours and terrible conditions endured by men like his father:

> Some of them started at 6 o'clock, it was a 12-hour day sometimes. Of a morning, there'd be a knock at the door 'ship's come'. My father'd have to get up, clothed and down to the ship.[20]

The wharves had few amenities, there were often no toilets or washing facilities, and breaks were short. Children like Fred were often given the task of taking meals down to their fathers:

(left to right) John 'Jack' Johnson, Thomas Hughes and sons Charlie and Fred (seated), c1915. Tenants No 58 Gloucester Street, 1915–31. Courtesy Cleo Grayson and Karen Moffatt **opposite** James 'Perc' Thompson with his son, Ron, c1934, taken by a street photographer. Tenants No 62 Gloucester Street, 1933–49. Courtesy Patricia Thomas

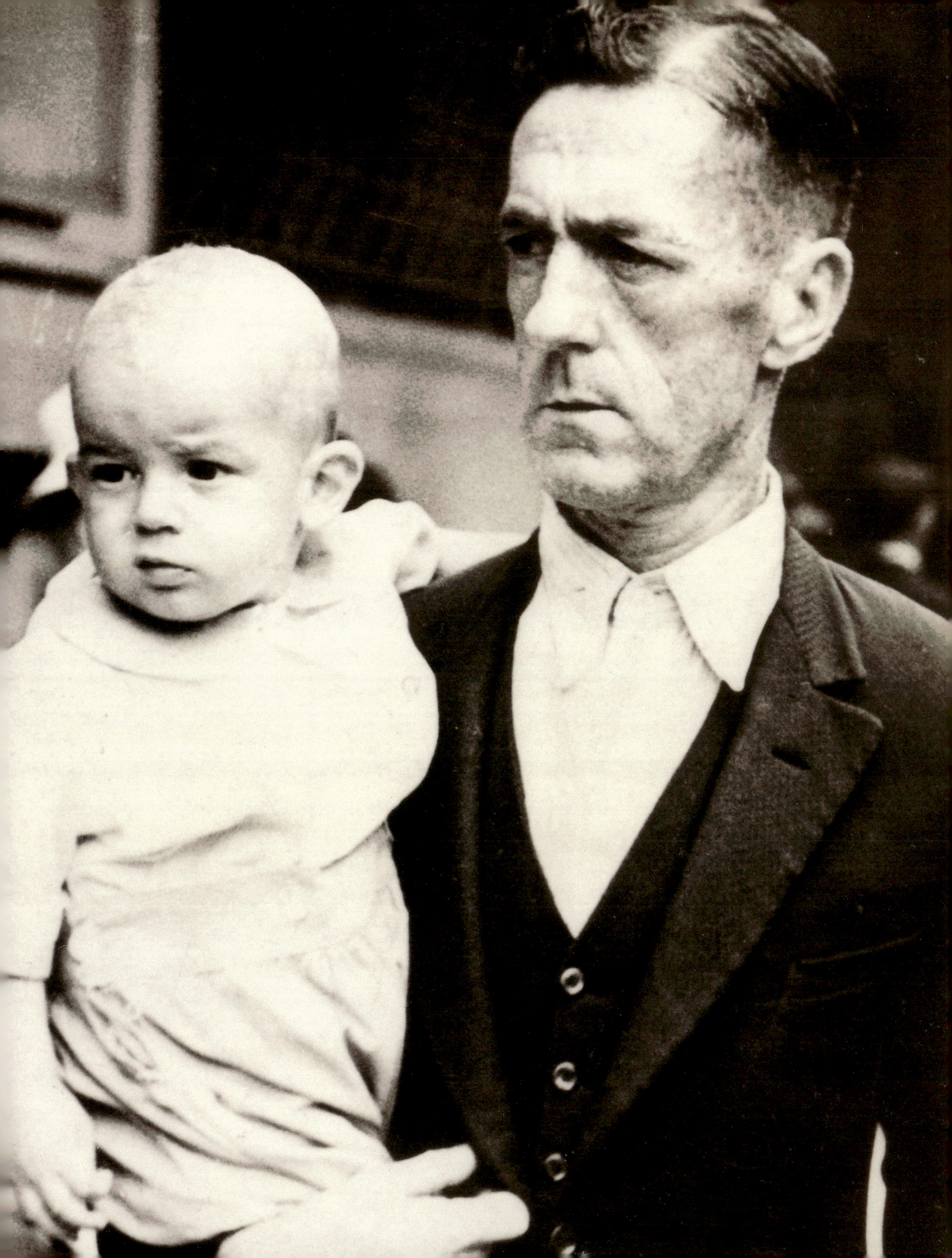

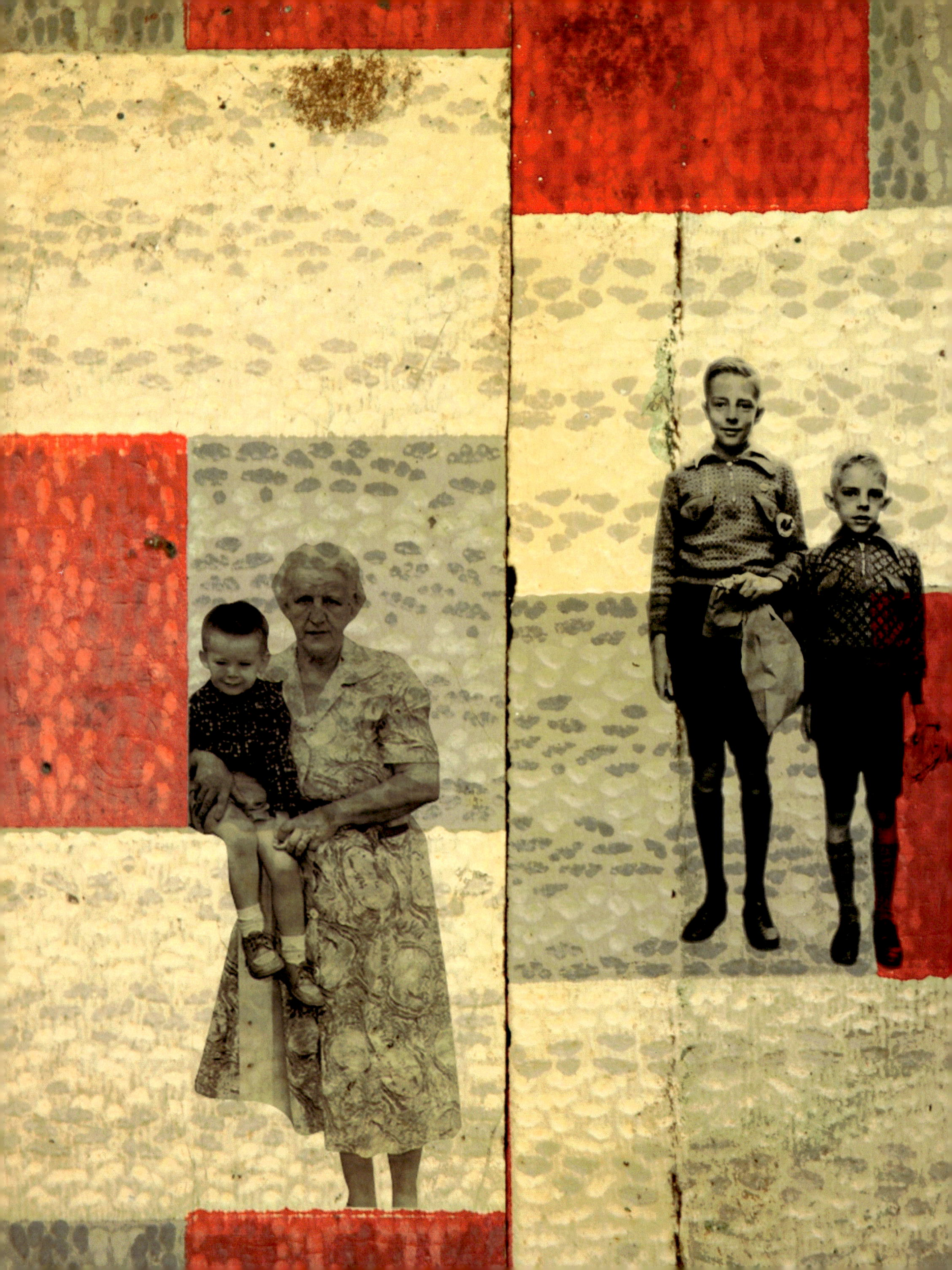

SHARED HISTORY, SEPARATE LIVES

Mum used to make sandwiches ... and when they worked alongside the wharf I used to take his meals down and we used to have a 'two plate' meal — a plate on top and bottom wrapped up with a tea towel.[21]

For many years the 'Bull system' operated, where men stood around the entrances to the wharves waiting to be picked by the clerks. Strong men were favoured while those who were rejected hurried on to the next wharf or missed a day's wages. The work was dangerous. One day someone had forgotten to put the plank out across the hull of a ship and Thomas Hughes stepped 'onto nothing', landing on the coal in the hull below. Thomas's injuries plagued him in later life and more than 70 years later Fred can still recall the 'little marks where the specks of coal dust' were embedded in the cuts on his father's skin.[22]

Many working-class families struggled to make ends meet, a situation made worse by the irregular nature of waterfront work and the huge rise in unemployment, homelessness and hunger. The Thompson family, with four children and another on the way, were forced to move from their relatively modern Federation tenements into the 90-year-old terrace that was Susannah Place. Although only four doors along in Gloucester Street, the move saved the family two shillings a week in rent.

At a time when married working women was unacceptable, women took in washing and lodgers and relied on their children as 'economic help' around the home.[23] At Susannah Place children looked after younger siblings, collected firewood and left school early to start work.

Rene McSherry and Bertha Hughes, c1920s. Hughes family tenants No 58 Gloucester Street, 1915–31. McSherry tenant No 58, 1931–32. Courtesy Cleo Grayson and Karen Moffatt **opposite left** Margaret Thompson with her grandson Paul, c1960s. Tenant No 62 Gloucester Street, 1933–42. Courtesy Patricia Thomas **right** Jack and Ernie Andersen, c1940s. Tenants No 58 and 64 Gloucester Street, 1939–74. Courtesy Jack Andersen **background** Linoleum c1953, No 64 Gloucester Street verandah kitchen, 2005, photograph © Ross Heathcote

PROGRESS NO.	DATE.		DATE OF REGISTRATION		
					62 Glouces
					193
31926	Apl	—	Apl	15	DR:- Rental arrears of
					193
32090	Dec	29	Dec.	30	H. O'Brien :- Requesting Electric ligh
					Will pay extra 1/6 per week rent

Mum washed on a Monday and she had the old copper stick and whoever walked past the copper used to pound the washing down. She used to light that copper underneath with bits of wood and coal. We used to search round the streets for the pieces of wood, old fruit boxes and cardboard and things like that to burn.[24]

Patricia Thomas, 1993. Tenant No 62 Gloucester Street, 1933–42

Patricia Thomas turned 14 on a Friday and the following Monday started work at a shirt factory. She gave her weekly pay of 12s 6d to her mother. Another former resident, Bertha Grayson, started to sew her own clothes at age 14 because her mother 'absolutely hated sewing … but she had to sew because she couldn't afford to go and buy all these ready-made things'.[25]

Before he left school Fred Hughes had permission to finish early on Fridays to work in Hugo Youngein's grocer shop. Many of the household chores also fell to the children; they scrubbed and swept the floors, chopped firewood, emptied the chamber pots, washed the dishes and went to the shops.

In 1918 a survey by Manchester City Council estimated that 'washing for a family of five took on average 9 hours and 29 minutes a week'.[26] The women of Susannah Place were still using the labour-intensive coppers for washing well into the 1960s. It is little wonder that after a day of this tiring and hot work, Lena Hughes used to give her son a billycan to get a quart of beer from the Australian Hotel. 'She'd drink the lot!' he recalled.[27] In the 1960s Beryl Smith, mother of three small children, had three jobs:

> I'd get up in the morning and go to Caltex House, start at 6 to 8 and come back at 9. Then I'd go to Playfairs from 9 to 3.30, then I'd take the kids and bath them and then go to the pub and work till 11. I only had one day, Sunday, off.[28]

Somehow, Beryl still found time to do the housework and cook the family's meals.

Raymond Smith posing in the billycart his father made, back lane (Cambridge Street), c1960s. Tenant No 64 Gloucester Street, 1956–72. Courtesy Ron Smith **background** No 62 Gloucester Street tenant card 1937–47, Sydney Harbour Foreshore Authority

When asked about the social networks in The Rocks, Patricia Thomas recalled, 'Men would see each other in the hotel … the women were always out talking. They'd have a little bit of a scandal and things like that'.[31] The children had their own domain in the laneways and footpaths. There were games of chasings, billycart rides, tea parties, skipping and, when the war was on, mock war games. They swam and fished in the harbour and played games at the King George V playground. As they grew older they took trips by ferry to Clifton Gardens, football games and movies at the cinemas in town.

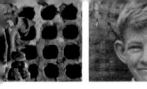

The fondest memories of many of Susannah Place's residents are those associated with the harbour. George Adaley never tired of the magnificent views from his uncle's bedroom window: 'As a young boy, I could get up there and focus my binoculars onto the quay and I could watch the ferries coming in'.[29] The Thompson family would hop on a Manly ferry to escape the hot summer nights: 'We used to … go backwards and forward … and when the war started and the blackouts was on all the lights used to go off on the ferry and it was a lovely trip'.[30]

Today many of these 'children' return to their former homes and neighbourhood with their own children and grandchildren, as do the descendants of the earliest tenants. With each visit come more memories; an emerging or untangling of a new thread of family history research. Yet despite the wealth of detail Susannah Place Museum has gathered, it affords only the smallest glimpse into the lives of our former residents; their stories, like the museum, are still in the making.

Fred Hughes (centre) with friends at Clifton Gardens, c1920s. Tenant No 58 Gloucester Street, 1915–31. Courtesy Cleo Grayson and Karen Moffatt **opposite left** Clara Youngein with sons James and John (seated) **right** Hugo Youngein with son Herbert and daughter Jenny, c1915. Tenants No 64 Gloucester Street, 1904–30. Susannah Place Museum Collection, Historic Houses Trust

I remember us all getting dressed to the nines to go up and have it [photograph] taken.[32]

James Young (Youngein), 1990. Tenant No 64 Gloucester Street, 1904–17

In the late 1940s some 'concerned' parents, worried their children 'were on the streets too much', started a social club on Saturday nights for local teenagers 'so that they won't be going out and getting into mischief'. Girlie and Martin Andersen in No 64 offered the use of their lounge room and charged three pence admission. Years later David Hamilton and Ron Thompson recalled these nights with a laugh: '... a record player and about two records and the lights would be out quite a lot of the time and there used to be lots of kissing'.[33]

Friends (left to right) David Hamilton, Ron Thompson and Ernie Andersen, photographed by a street photographer in town, late 1940s, Susannah Place Museum Collection, Historic Houses Trust **background** No 64 Gloucester Street tenant card 1932–34, Sydney Harbour Foreshore Authority

64 Gloucester St

PROGRESS NO.	DATE.	DATE OF REGISTRATION	
			1932
32136	June 9	June 10	Eng. renovations to Moma

32668	Oct 23	Oct 24	C. Snedden: Asking installa
			1934
31879	May 10	May 14	C. Commins: Notice to repair
32393	Aug 13	Aug 13	p.
32394		13	p. Drawing attention to Painting Cl

SHARED HISTORY, SEPARATE LIVES

left Amelia Stewart, c1900. Tenant and grocer of No 64 Gloucester Street, 1901–03. Susannah Place Museum Collection, Historic Houses Trust **top right** (left to right) Ernie Andersen, Billy Pinder, David Hamilton, Mr Pinder and Tommy Smith, c1950s. Courtesy Terri Williams **bottom right** Lena Hughes (far left) and daughter Bertha (in bathing costume), c1930s. Tenants No 58 Gloucester Street, 1915–31. Courtesy Cleo Grayson and Karen Moffatt

left Mary 'Girlie' (Andersen) with parents, Adelaide and John Gallagher, and her first husband, Walter Curran, c1927. Courtesy Terri Williams
top right (left to right) Ernie Andersen and his parents, Girlie and Martin, and family friend, c1950s. Courtesy Jack Andersen **bottom right** (left to right) Jeffrey Smith, Shelley Nolan, Kristine Smith and Susie Campbell in the backyard of No 62 Gloucester Street, c1960s. Courtesy Ron Smith

THE
RED CROWN
RESTAURANT
DINING ROOMS.
HERE ONLY
WALK IN & JUDGE FOR YOURSELF
ROAST PORK FOUR TIMES A WEEK
21
13/6
6D
BREAKFAST A SPECIALITY
CUT LUNCHES
21 TICKETS
14/6
CIGARETTES SOLD HERE
606

SHARED HISTORY, SEPARATE LIVES

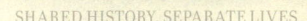

1. Sali Herman from an interview in Brian Turner, *The Australian terrace house*, Angus & Robertson, Sydney, 1995, p83.
2. Paul Thompson, *The voice of the past: oral histories*, 1978, back cover.
3. Flo Gallagher quoted in Robert Griffin, 'Life at Susannah Place' [brochure], Historic Houses Trust, Sydney, c1995.
4. Jack and Shirly Andersen oral history, 1992.
5. Patricia Thomas (nee O'Brien/Thompson) oral history, 1993.
6. Fred Hughes and Bertha Grayson (nee Hughes) oral history, 1994.
7. *The Rocks at Federation: photographs from the C H Bertie Collection*, Sydney Cove Authority, 1998, p19.
8. Insolvency file of William Thomas Merchant, 18 January 1872, State Records NSW: Supreme Court, CGS 13654, Insolvency Files, 1842–87, File No 10887.
9. S Mossman & T Banister, *Australia, visited and revisited. A narrative of recent travels and old experiences in Victoria and New South Wales*, Ure Smith in assn with the National Trust of Australia (NSW), Sydney, 1974, pp203–06 (originally published by Addey & Co, London, 1853).
10. *The West Briton*, 3 February 1837.
11. Fred Hughes oral history, 1992.
12. Jean Ritchie, *Lizzie's Farm at North Curl Curl*, Book House, Sydney, 1999, p15.
13. George Adaley and Kay Kallas oral history, 1993.
14. City Improvement Advisory Board, *Report on the operations of the City Improvement Advisory Board*, Public Works Department Annual Report 1902/03, p52.
15. Select Committee on the Condition of the Working Classes of the Metropolis, Minutes of evidence, *Votes and Proceedings of the Legislative Assembly of New South Wales, 1859–60*, vol 4, p2946.
16. Fred Hughes oral history, 1992.
17. Ron Thompson and David Hamilton oral history, 2001.
18. ibid
19. Leslie Poynter oral history, 1993.
20. Fred Hughes oral history, 1992.
21. Fred Hughes and Bertha Grayson oral history, 1994.
22. Fred Hughes oral history, 1992.
23. Shirley Fitzgerald and Christopher Keating, *Millers Point: the urban village*, Hale & Iremonger, Sydney, 1991, pp93–4.
24. Patricia Thomas oral history, 1993.
25. Fred Hughes and Bertha Grayson oral history, 1994.
26. Chris Upton, *Living back-to-back*, Phillimore & Co Ltd, West Sussex, 2005, p86.
27. Fred Hughes oral history, 1992.
28. Beryl Smith (nee Kidd) oral history, 1993.
29. George Adaley and Kay Kallas oral history, 1993.
30. Patricia Thomas oral history, 1993.
31. ibid
32. James Young (Youngein) oral history, 1990.
33. Ron Thompson and David Hamilton oral history, 2001.

left Oilcloth, c1900s, No 58 Gloucester Street front room, 2005, photograph © Ross Heathcote **centre** Raymond and Joan Naylor 1951. Tenants No 60 Gloucester Street, 1951–52. Courtesy Joan Killen **right** Toilet door, No 64 Gloucester Street (detail), 2004, photograph © Ross Heathcote **opposite** Colonial Cafe, operated by Emmanuel Sarantides (far right), c1920s. Courtesy Kay Kallas

TENANTS LIST

No 58

James and Mary McHill [Hill]	1845–55
Thomas Martin	1857
William Murray	1858
John Rule	1861
William McCarthy	1865–66
Mrs Mary McCarthy and Hugh and Eugene McCarthy	1867–71
John and Mary Rule	1873–82, 1884–86
H Moorehausen	1883
George and Martha Lindon	1887–99
William Rule	1901
John Moran	1902
John McCarthy	1904
William and Mary Akehurst	1906–14
John Henry Mullen	1913
Robert John Brunyee	1915–17
John Eric Johnson	1915–16, 1925–30
Annie O'Toole	1915–17
Thomas and Lena Pearl Hughes and children Charles, Fred, Bertha, Iris	1915–31
Christian Swanson	1916–17
William Jones	1925–26
Annie White	1926
Jane E Aubin	1931
Mrs McSherry	1931–32
John Gallagher	1932
Mrs Edmondson	1933
John and Adelaide 'Ada' Gallagher	1934–49
Leslie and Florence Gallagher and daughter Gloria	1944
Emily Curtis	1949–51, 1953
Arnt 'Martin' and Mary 'Girlie' Andersen	1949–64
Ernie Andersen	1949–74
Jack and Shirly Andersen	1950–54
Gordon Gallagher	1963
Pamela Andersen and son David	1968–70

No 60

Francis and Ellen Cunninghame	1845–46
Bridget Norton	1847–48
Robert Grace	1848–51
Joseph Hume	1853–55
Henry Whitehall	1857
John Jones	1858
Denis Baragray	1861
William Thomas Merchant	1865
James Hogan	1867–68
Mrs Parsonage	1870
John Rule	1871
James and Mary Ann Warlow	1873
William and Bridget Merchant	1875–84
William Marsh	1884
Robert and Mary Jane Bell	1885–93
Alfred H Miller	1894
James Moodie	1895–96
Denis and Mary McClafferty	1897–1904
David and Alice Hogan	1906–08
Charles Smith	1906
Henry and Mary Clark	1908–09
Alice Herbert	1909, 1913–17
William and Mary Sharp	1909–13
George and Lizzie Sayce	1909–10
Mary Herbert	1910–17
Sydney James and Caroline Morton	1913
John Jenkins	1919
Elizabeth Ritchie	1920–21
Annie Poynter	1921–22
Margaret Doyle and Thomas McNamara	1925–33
Peter Theodor	1936–40
Rose, Emmanuel and Athas 'Arthur' Sarantides	1936–46
Dimitrios and Maria Passaris	1947
Robert Bede Craig	1949–50

Bessie Naylor and son Raymond	1949–50
Raymond and Joan Naylor	1951–52
Raymond and Ken Hunt	1955
Esther Maud Moran and son Walter	1953–68

No 62

Thomas Hall	1845
Edward and Mary Riley (owners)	1846–74
George Hill	1876–77
Edward and Janet Dudgeon	1879–80
William Detuerner	1882
John and Margaret White	1883–88
Alfred Henry and Eliza Miller	1889–93
Mrs McClafferty	1894
Mrs Fanny Dawes	1897–98
John Lester	1900
Bernard Fisher	1901–02
Richard and Mary Fauld	1904–06
Chas Pack	1908
Michael Curran	1908–09
Arthur and Elizabeth Smith	1909–31
Ada Elizabeth Smith	1913
William Boshell	1921
Alexander Simula	1921
Sydney Smith	1926–28
Mabel Elizabeth Smith	1928–30
Lucy Clayson	1931–33
Rosina and William Howard	1931–33
James 'Perc' and Margaret Thompson and children Patricia, Mercia, Colleen and Ron	1933–42 (James until 1949)
Albert and Maureen Thompson	1949–61
Noel Banfield	1958–62
Ellen and Dennis Marshall and Ellen's daughter Jenni (Whitford)	1962–90
Anna Cossu and Geoff Marsh (museum caretakers)	1995–2006

No 64

John Munro	1845
Patrick Ryan	1847–48
Joseph and Sarah Musgrave	1851–55
John Taylor	1857
Croft Fulstow and Mary Ann Hall	1858–70
George McIntyre	1871–73
John Thames [James Thomas]	1875
John and Mary Anne Finnegan (owners)	1876–77
George Hill	1879–98
James Gallagher	1899–1900
Peter and Amelia Stewart	1901–03
Hugo and Clara Youngein and children Jenny, James, John and Herbert	1904–30
Sarah McKinley	1908
Eliza and Robert Sneddon	1931–35
Robert McMorran	1933–34
Maude Lillian Hickey	1936
Arnt 'Martin' and Mary 'Girlie' Andersen and children Ernie and Jack	1937–49
Leo Francis Brown	1939–46
Mary Carmichael	1949–54
John Sneddon Peace	1951–54
Margaret and Maurice Toppenberg	1954–55
Beryl and Ronald Smith	1956–65
Donald Kidd	1959–63
Jean and Norman Philpott	1965–70
Ronald Smith	1965–72

This list has been compiled from official records and oral history interviews and is current as of September 2007. Research is ongoing and this list is regularly updated to reflect new information.

The list does not include all the names of the children from each family and the end date is the date that the last member of the family left the property.

FURTHER READING

Charles Bertie, *Old Sydney*, Angus & Robertson Ltd, Sydney, 1911

Max Kelly, *Anchored in a small cove: a history and archaeology of The Rocks, Sydney*, Sydney Cove Authority, Sydney, 1997

Grace Karskens, *The Rocks: life in early Sydney*, Melbourne University Press, Melbourne, 1997

Grace Karskens, *Inside the Rocks: the archaeology of a neighbourhood*, Hale & Iremonger, Sydney, 1999

Eliza Walker & S K Johnstone, 'Old Sydney in the 'forties: recollections of Lower George Street and "The Rocks"', *Journal of the Royal Australian Historical Society*, vol 16, 1930

ACKNOWLEDGMENTS

This book would not have been possible without the generosity and ongoing support of the former tenants and their descendants. They have allowed us into their lives, shared their memories, loaned photographs, donated objects and answered endless questions about life at Susannah Place. And, most graciously of all, they let us share their stories with visitors to the museum.

To my colleagues at the Historic Houses Trust, special thanks to Anne-Louise Falson whose beautiful book design so wonderfully captures the essence of the houses and to Vani Sripathy for her patience and guidance as editor. Many thanks to Annie Eyers for her unfailing support, dogged research and endless hours of discussion, which invariably and happily led to new avenues of research. Many thanks also to Sue Hunt for her ideas and encouragement and Ross Heathcote for his wonderful close-up studies of the houses that beautifully illustrate this book. Thanks also to Christopher Shain who over the years has documented the houses and people of Susannah Place.

I am also grateful to Susan Sedgwick for keeping the book on track, Alice Livingstone for all her work on copyright and image collection and Rhiain Hull for the final stages of editing. For their assistance and support thanks also to Louise Cornwall, Matthew Stephens, Penny Gill, Margaret Shain, Trudi Fletcher, Alda Scofield, Peter Barnes and Caroline Mackaness.

At the Sydney Harbour Foreshore Authority I would like to thank Dr Wayne Johnson who is always generous with his time and knowledge of The Rocks and Lynda Kelly for finding those elusive images.

Lastly, and most of all, thanks to Geoff Marsh whose wise words, love and support were essential to this book.

Anna Cossu